19

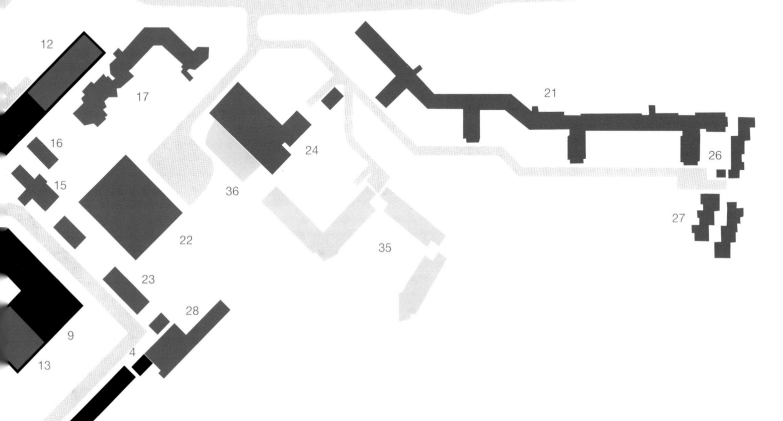

12

17

16

15

22

23

28

9

13

4

3

19

21

24

36

35

26

27

**Rick Mather Associates:**

| 30 | Education | 1982-1984 |
|----|-----------|-----------|
| 31 | Information Systems | 1983-1985 |
| 32 | Climatic Research | 1984-1985 |

**Foster Associates:**

| 29 | Sainsbury Centre | 1974-1978 |
|----|------------------|-----------|

**Foster Associates:**

| 33 | Sainsbury Centre Crescent Wing | 1989-1991 |
|----|--------------------------------|-----------|

**Rick Mather Associates:**

| 34 | Constable Terrace | 1992-1993 |
|----|-------------------|-----------|
| 35 | Nelson Court | 1991-1993 |
| 36 | Drama Studio | 1992-1994 |

**John Miller & Partners:**

| 37 | Queen's Building | 1992-1994 |
|----|------------------|-----------|
| 38 | Elizabeth Fry Building | 1993-1995 |

# CONCRETE AND OPEN SKIES

Architecture at the University of East Anglia 1962-2000

# CONCRETE AND OPEN SKIES

## Architecture at the University of East Anglia 1962-2000

Peter Dormer and Stefan Muthesius

UNICORN PRESS

LONDON

Unicorn Press
76 Great Suffolk Street
London SE1 0BL

email: unicorn@tradford.demon.co.uk

First published by Unicorn Press, 2001

ISBN 0 906290 60 0

Designed by Jonathan Raimes, Foundation Publishing Ltd
Printed in Slovenia

Cover: **The University from Bluebell Road.**
Frontispiece: **Norfolk Terrace and Teaching Wall,**
**by Denys Lasdun and David Luckhurst, 1966, 1973.**

# CONTENTS

# ACKNOWLEDGMENTS

This book begins with a record of sadness. In 1994/5 Peter Dormer joined the School of World Art Studies and Museology as the holder of a treble fellowship: of the Eastern Arts Council, of the Crafts Council, as well as of the University itself. What Peter brought to the School in that lively year was a rare combination of trustworthy history and insightful criticism. There was a consensus that, as an eminent historian of Modernist design and as a respected architectural journalist for *The Independent*, Peter Dormer was the right person to help with writing an account of UEA's architectural history. But his share of the book was to be his last work. Peter died of cancer on 24th December 1996. Since then the text has been reorganised several times but to those who knew him and remember his work, his ideas and his style, the spirit of the friendly critical investigator will shine through many of these pages.

Naturally, the authors owe a great deal to all those who have been prepared to speak to them at length, but none more so than Peter Yorke, who worked in the university administration almost from its earliest days and who later on oversaw much of the building activities. In fact Peter Yorke very early on turned from interviewee to 'informant' and elucidator. Much of the technical detail, as well as many of the more general insights are owed to him.

The 'Seven' new universities of the 1960s vary greatly as to the degree of self-consciousness. UEA belongs to those who have so far hesitated to record and communicate their evolution. But such a work is now forthcoming. The historian Michael Sanderson's help and understanding has been most valuable in the course of our work. Michael Brandon-Jones's photographic work has been crucial, not only in this book, but in many others. Photographs that enter his studio always leave it improved. Special thanks are also due to Matthew Moran (editing work) Deirdre Sharp (UEA Library, Archives), Michael Paulson-Ellis and Alan Preece, (organisation and funding), Christopher Smith in general, as well as Joseph Saunders who is now 'in charge' of UEA's architecture on the University's side.

Among the others who have to be thanked most are Ken Adcock (R.G.Carter Ltd.), Joe Aldous, Marjorie Allthorp-Guyton, Sarah Beatty, Richard Brearley, Ian Brooke, Alison Brown, Hannah Brown, Derek Burke, Amanda Chenery-Howes, Sarah Cocke, Sir Timothy Colman, Edward Cullinan, Rosemary Dixon, Dame Elizabeth Esteve-Coll, Sir Bernard M.Feilden, Lord Norman Foster, Joe Geitner, Richard Goodall, Fiona Grant, Willi Guttsman, Rowan Hare, Christopher Harper-Bill, Tanya Harrod, Robert Haynes, Sandy Heslop, C.Hewlett, Miles Glendinning, Mike Hollingworth, Ludmilla Jordanova, Sue Koria, Sir Denys Lasdun (also Peter McKinley and Alexander Redhouse), Robin Lucas, Derek Lummis, James Macfarlane, Ray Matthias, Cliff Middleton, Victor Morgan, Evelyn Mould, Joanna Motion, Katarzyna Murawska-Muthesius, Michal Murawski, Bianca Muthesius, Martyn Newton, Anne Ogden, Bohdan Paczowski, Frances Pearce, Patricia Porritt, Vic Purdy, Ros Pye, Lady Enid Ralphs, Marjorie Ralphs, Catherine Reynolds, Marjorie Rhodes, John Richardson, Norah Rogers, Derek Sang, Stella Shackle, Jane Smith, Peter Smith, Sir Arthur South, Marcelle Steller-Caudley, Gordon Tilsley, Anne-Marie Triggs, Wally Tyacke, Professor Emeritus Frank Thistlethwaite, Norma Watt, Vincent Watts, Patricia Whitt, Nick Zurbrugg, my colleagues present and past and the students in my School, as well as Colin Bunn, Stan Davies and their colleagues.

# PREFACE

The aim of this book is strictly, even unashamedly, architectural. It addresses the users and the visitors and says to them: this is how the buildings are, and, crucially, this is what they look like; this is how striking they are ('beautiful' was too controversial a word in the twentieth century), or at least intriguing, or, at the very least, this is what the buidlings are 'characteristic of ...'. While for an architect it is his or her business to create a striking look, and a new look, from the clients or patrons this demands immense conviction, to allow vast sums of money to be spent on something that has not been tried before. Much of the text, therefore, deals with issues of patronage. However, it was not just the 'look' the patrons were after, they entertained political, social, moral, educational, as well as academic values which they hoped would somehow be embodied in the forms of the buildings. It was this intended fusion of form and content which characterises the older architecture of a campus like UEA, during the 'heroic' periods of the 1960s and 70s. What this book does not want to provide, however, is a hagiography. The story of single-mindedness is usually also a story of problems. In the end, much of the meaning of architecture is derived in the (historical) explanation of the problems prevalent in its creation and the perceived problems in the process of its reception.

That said, it is our belief that the architectural past of a single institution is best understood when it is approached from the present. Being aimed at those who experience the buildings now, and their sense of history, it is hoped that this approach can balance somewhat the 'hard' intentionalism of the founders and make the whole undertaking appear a more user-friendly one. However, like many histories, this book stops short of the actual present and the near future. The Greater University of the year 2000 and the way it reaches beyond the old institutionality in terms of its activities and in terms of its newest buildings and plans for the future, cannot be dealt with here. Our subject is the development of UEA's main campus. Starting with the sophisticated but gentle architecture of the early 1990s, this might also be taken as a general introduction, in so much as it allows us to appreciate, by contrast, the heroism and the brutalism of the distant 1960s and 1970s. The University's two major early phases, Sainsbury/Foster and Thistlethwaite/Lasdun/Feilden are treated as self-contained stories. Beyond that, the first beginnings of UEA now really do belong to 'history'; few people are around who remember them, and the best loved of all UEA's building complexes, the 'Village', is long gone. In the last chapter the book takes on some more general issues of patronage and architectual meaning in the context of the region.

Following pages, left: **Main stairs in the Elizabeth Fry Building (with Peter Yorke, UEA's Acting/Deputy Buildings Officer 1988-96).** Right: **Queen's Building, cycle shed.**

# I  FROM THE GREATER UNIVERSITY OF 2000 BACK TO THE 1990s AND 1980s

## SAVING ENERGY WITH ELEGANCE: MILLER AND MATHER

Before beginning a discourse on 'architectural innovations', it may be appropriate to try to assess how many of the day-to-day users of the campus would normally reflect on these matters. In the era of heroic university planning of the 1960s, some commentators could rhapsodise: 'The new University Movement... as exciting as the cathedral building movement of the early twelfth century ...'. Such language would clearly cut no ice today. Most users are glad if their immediate working environment is functioning reasonably well. When it comes to the campus as a whole, what is uppermost in people's minds is simply how to get to their place of work. Today, car parking appears by far the most serious issue in campus design. This brings us straight to a major criticism of UEA's plan, and much of the criticism goes back to the way in which Denys Lasdun and the University estimated, in the 1960s, a modest 25 % of car users; while he thought 'for the rest of the population... there is ample cycle parking'. Today's critics, however, ought to bear in mind that UEA's out of town campus is still relatively compact and that in a 'multiversity' of the same size situated in a town the distances could be very much greater.

'Planning', in the year 2000, has a different sense when compared with its meaning in the Lasdun period of the 1960s. Then, a 'plan' entailed a strong overall ethos and especially a conviction of utter newness which today it would be difficult to even imagine. But when examining recent aerial photographs and also when we keep our eyes close to the ground, we have to admit that we are not disturbed by much that is unfinished or untidy. This is, of course, the result of watchful and competent maintenance, but it mainly stems from a comprehensive recent plan by Rick Mather, the University's most important designer of the 1980s and 90s. In anticipation of UEA's expansion, in 1987, the then Vice-Chancellor Derek Burke commissioned Mather to produce a Development Plan. This represents the most incisive analysis of the campus to date, with a strong emphasis on the visual. Mather began by agreeing with Denys Lasdun's basic contention that, in order to preserve the constant interpenetration of

Below: **Denys Lasdun (1963): The extendible university: Year 3, 5, 7, 10, 15.**
Right: **The campus, late 1990s.**

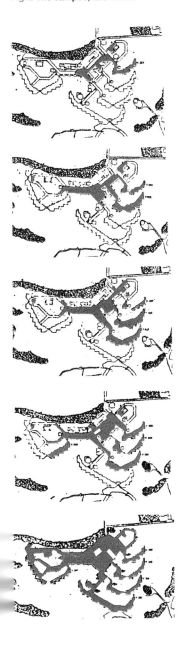

architecture and landscape, there is little available space for new buildings. What is perhaps more surprising is that Mather continues Lasdun's splendid isolationism: 'Where suburban housing along Bluebell Road intrudes into the campus and destroys the precious illusion that the University is set in parkland and country, tree settings should be planted as soon as possible'. Buildings must be placed selectively, and in such a way as to continue the east-west axis of the complex. Mather further tidied up the 'backlands' on the northern flank of the Teaching Wall by cutting a straight road through the area. This is meant to be lined with more buildings on both sides. Beyond that, landscaping for Mather implied the greatest care for the immediate surroundings of buildings; it is its pathways, cycle stands, sunken areas and planting which gives the University a degree of neatness that it never possessed before. Mather also greatly improved Feilden's backland behind the Student Union through landscaping and with the addition of the Drama Studio (1991-4). Another achievement of Mather's and his successor's, Miller, is the way in which the Queen's Building and the Elizabeth Fry Building, together with the northern face of Mather's Constable Terrace, form a large, almost enclosed space, a court, or 'urban' square, as one is inclined to call it. The designers even managed to arrange the parking in a neat fashion. UEA, then, is a rare instance of a campus without 'back' areas, or messy back entrances. Not all, however, was harmony. In one case the diversity of UEA's architecture produced an impasse. Miller's last project was for the Norfolk Record Office, planned as a 'wrap-round' building, closely flanking two sides of Lasdun's Library. According to one's viewpoint, the old stood in the way of the new, or the new could not fit in with the old. In the end, grants were not forthcoming for a number of reasons.

The chief merits of UEA's architecture of the last two decades do not, however, lie within an overall scheme, but with each individual building. Today's capital costs are rarely funded by the central state; a university has to fight anew for each building to find funds from varied sources; the Queen's Building, for instance, was paid for by the Regional Health Authority. 'The Teaching Wall', so an architectural critic on recent UEA buildings has remarked, 'could have been extended or altered with ease; instead, today's requirements are for smaller, stand-alone buildings'. What buildings are expected to provide today is a painstaking response to a great diversity of user requirements, and to do so with varied forms and a high degree of finish. The contrast with Lasdun's Teaching Wall, in its crushing uniformity, could not be greater. UEA's new buildings were contributed by two firms, Miller and Mather; the latter's career we will highlight later when he enters UEA in the 1980s. John Miller & Partners were, in fact, brought in by Mather. (The Elizabeth Fry Building was won in a limited competition with Mather and Feilden & Mawson). This firm, under the name Colquhoun & Miller had been in business for considerably longer than Mather's, although their's was hardly a household name in English post-war architecture. At UEA the partner in charge was Richard Brearley. Miller's is an image of 'discretion'; their forms are largely derived from

International Modern whiteness of the 1920s. The firm's masterpiece, up to that point, was the extension of the London Whitechapel Art Gallery of 1985, immensely complex and carefully detailed, though little of its exterior can actually be seen. As with Mather, the firm's buildings in Norwich constituted their most important job to date.

Neither Queen's nor Elizabeth Fry can be called cramped, but for the first time architects at UEA were faced with tight plots. Queen's responds directly to Mather's Education School, by reciprocating the latter's open courtyard. Elizabeth Fry had to be extended along Mather's new straight road. Above all, both buildings have extremely complex requirements: Elizabeth Fry alone is said to have 37 kinds of rooms and can serve 1300 users simultaneously, in lecture rooms, seminar rooms, offices, complex foyers with art display areas and other spaces. The co-operation of client and designer was very close. Much attention is given to the energy aspect which Mather had introduced a few years before in his student residences. But while Mather saved heat very much through squareness and compactness and through reducing the size of the windows, there seemed to be no need to resort to this in Miller's buildings. Their architecure appears as open and varied in its plans as one would expect of a friendly public institution today. Queen's especially plays boldly with the interpenetration of exterior and interior space. And yet the heat loss, especially in Elizabeth Fry, is even lower than Mather could achieve. Triple-glazed windows came straight from Sweden, as did the 'Termodek System', with hollowed-out concrete floor slabs filled with either cool night air, or warm air according to the time of the year. The heating capacity needed for the whole building is no more than that of an ordinary semi-detached house. As Andy Ford of Fulcrum Engineering Partnership put it: 'The approach must be that the quality of building construction comes first and building services second, with every step in the heat exchange route checked for efficiency'. Equally important was the task to introduce 'comfort cooling' (Brearley) without mechanical chilling. A long testing of the occupied Elizabeth Fry Building, undertaken by the independent Building Research Establishment, resulted in the claim that it was, at the time, the most energy efficient institutional building in Britain. As already mentioned, contemporary buildings of this kind are conceived as 'stand-alone' (from Mather's Education School onwards), that is, independent of the campus central service systems. The 1960s thinking: comprehensive heating (with the Central Boiler House) now seems old-fashioned.

It is Miller's detailing that takes in the observer. It was perhaps natural that both buildings, devoted, as they are, to health subjects and social work, had to look white and smooth. Whiteness is a trademark of the firm in any case. In fact, there is also much grey (tending towards a warm, brownish grey) and some black. The chief impression of the interior is of being well lit throughout. A number of historical sources suggest themselves: stark 1920s Modernism made to look precious; an English pre-

Vice Chancellor Derek Burke (1987-95) under the centre of Constable Terrace, which he commissioned Rick Mather to design in 1989.

High Modernist linearity and the external heaviness of an early 1950s Royal Festival Hall kind (indeed, Miller once worked with Sir Leslie Martin); a Post-Modernist sense of geometrical patterning, such as framed circles, and finally a restrained High-Tech style of delicate and inventive metal parts. Yet by no means does all this result in a sense of luxury and expense - one only needs to glance to Foster's Crescent Wing across the way. Brearley's 'high detailing' is achieved through the judicious avoidance of mere blank walls, through the regular occurrence of circular forms, through proportioning and subtle variations of colour, as well as clever lighting partly hidden in the coved ceilings. The furniture is mostly of solid wood in a Scandinavian/Arts & Crafts style. By comparison with all this immense sophistication and resplendent cleanliness, Mather's work of 1984, with his stronger greys and metallic blues already looks a little dark and slightly aged.

It was in the early 1990s that the University began once more to expand rapidly, virtually doubling its students numbers between 1986-94, to 7500. Building activity again approached the peak of the 1960s. Priority was given to student residences, but some more up-market suites for guests were also included. Of this most variable type of university building, UEA already possessed a large number of markedly different solutions. Mather carefully tried to emulate the main form of the campus, and so his two blocks are rather elongated, Constable Terraces meandering in a double curve, Nelson Court in an angular, but not rectangular, fashion, echoing the form of Waveney Terrace of the 1970s. In all other respects Mathers residences differ completely from previous ones (except for, at UEA, the small groups of Orwell and Wolfson Close, pages 120-1). The four-storey structure is divided into 'houses', forming, in fact, a terrace of houses; each front door provides access to ten rooms on three floors, with a ground-floor common room which gives out, via large windows, on to the pathway in front, into a little forecourt, with benches. Here Mather takes up ideas that date back to the 1950s and 1960s, to the Smithsons and their attempts to link public open and semi-private areas around the threshold of the house or flat; sources which to some extent also lay behind Lasdun's residences - though the differences between Mather and Lasdun could not be more striking. The top floor of Mather's blocks resorts to the more usual hostel type of central corridor access, though it is enlivened, in typical Mather fashion, with curved walls and circular roof lights.

What is not immediately apparent is the tightly-enclosed square block-like character of these buildings. The windows are of the legally permitted minimum size and the way in which they lie flush to the wall surface increases the sense of impenetrability. The primary aim, of course, is the opposite: to keep heat inside the building. Constable Terrace and Nelson Court were claimed to be Britain's largest and most important energy-saving residential buildings at the time they were built. Apart from 'sealing the building, this is achieved through a system of mechanical ventilation, whereby the heat which is contained in the extracted air, and which was produced largely by body heat, cooking etc., is used to heat incoming fresh air; 'heat recovery', or, in other words, the occupants heat their rooms themselves! The estimated cost of heating was 60 % of halls built in the 1970s. It is not surprising that a detailed description of the buildings and their construction reads like the accounts of scientific experiments, with a long list of unusual materials and proprietary components. And yet, we are assured that none of these incurred exceptional expense.

There seemed no way here in which Mather could indulge in the spatial fantasies of his 1980s Education building. But he does not dispense with elaborate staircases; now he puts them on the outside. In Nelson Court they are placed at the angles of the building; and although they are glazed they are not heated. There is also much decoration on the corners of the building, and at the top we find a kind of projecting lid, lit from below, which recalls Mather's sleek London bars and restaurants.

Mather's interiors, we read in the *Journal of Royal Institute of British Architects*, 'are of an incredibly high standard' - and that, we have to remember, at a relatively low price. Of Miller's Queen's Building the critic Robert Maxwell said that it 'has an aura of being careful to people'. However, on the basis of a 1996 RIBA survey of 31 recent buildings for higher education institutions in England, there seems no reason to doubt that at least a good number of them are of the same high quality as those at UEA. Certainly none of them appear dull, or overbearing, or brutal, nor do we learn about serious practical deficiencies. When judging some of the older buildings on UEA's campus, many would claim that there are those which may be exciting or intriguing to look at, but in many respects awkward to use, while the reverse might apply to some others: good to use but unappealing visually. Today's architectural production seems to exclude such vexing oppositions. New forms of organization, such as the management contract, move far beyond the old sequence of presenting a complete design first and then selecting a builder. Briefs are now devised by groups of specialists, those representing the users and the paymasters, as well as the designers and the building component suppliers, and from an early stage there is communication with the contractor. 'Design' has somewhat changed in meaning, coming closer to 'detailing', and is thus moving away from the essentialism in the grand concepts of High and late Modernism. In other words, today the processes are more predictable and more subject to control throughout. As we shall see, the projects of the 1960s proceeded by first conceiving the 'ultimate' combination of educational ethos and architectural form on a vast scale, followed by the 'buccaneering' patron/client, the vice-chancellor and his coterie intent on 'pushing through' 'their' scheme; the details followed at a later stage. Even in the mid-1980s, in Mather's Education and Systems building, we meet a more idiosyncratic overall sense of architecture.

Comparing the interior of Feilden & Mawson's Administration Building (the Registry, left) of the early 1970s with the same kind of space in the Elizabeth Fry Building (above) of the early 1990s is like comparing the comforts and looks of two reasonably-priced cars of those respective periods.

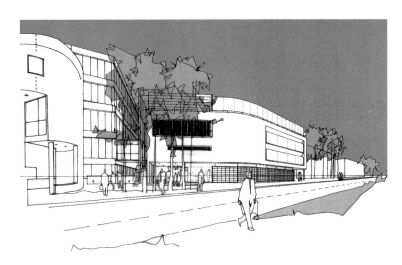

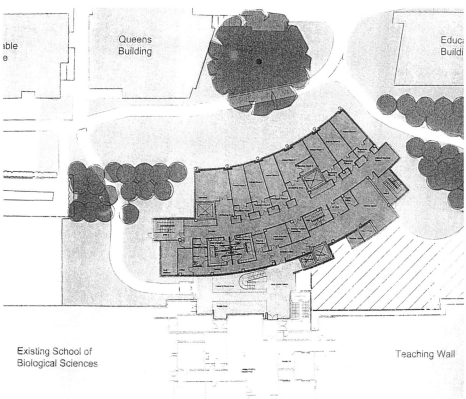

Queens Building

Educa
Buildi

able
e

Existing School of
Biological Sciences

Teaching Wall

Clockwise from top left: **ICER Building** (Institute
for Connective Environmental Research),
project 1999 by Robert Mathew Johnson-
Marshall (RMJM).
**APB Building** (Animal, Plant and Bacterial
Research Centre), proposal 1999 by RH
Partnership (Cambridge).
**UEA Sports Park,** built 1997-2000 by Willmott
Dixon / RH Partnership (Cambridge).
Project for Norfolk Record Office alongside
University Library, J.Miller & Partners, 1996
(abandoned).

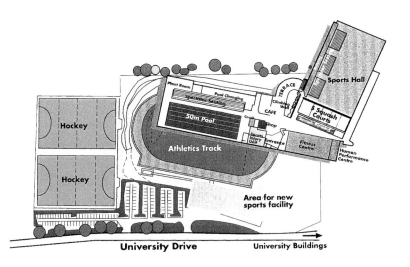

The Queen's Building, by J.Miller & Partners
1992-4.

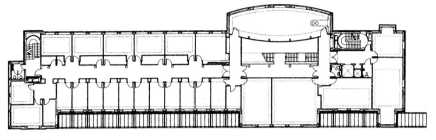

**FIRST FLOOR PLAN**

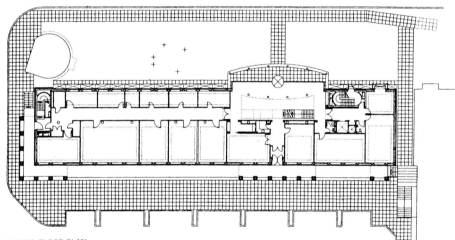

**GROUND FLOOR PLAN**

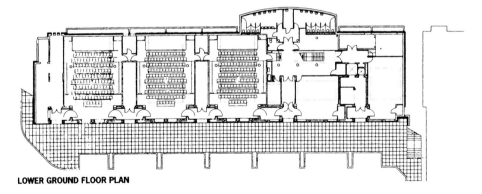

**LOWER GROUND FLOOR PLAN**

Left: Elizabeth Fry Building, by J. Miller & Partners, 1993-5, contains lecture theatres and seminar rooms for the use of many Schools, as well as offices for the School of Social Work and the School of Health Policy and Practice.

Below: The Queen's Building, opened in 1994 by Queen Elizabeth II, serves the School of Occupational Therapy and Physiotherapy. Plan of first floor.

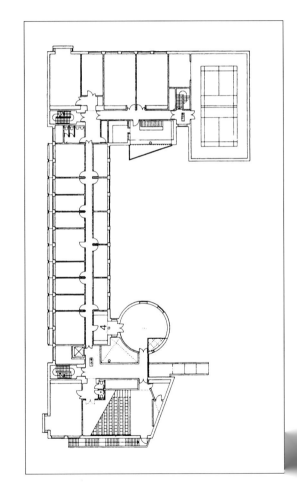

Elizabeth Fry Building, northern facade.
Right: Elizabeth Fry Building, foyer and main staircase.

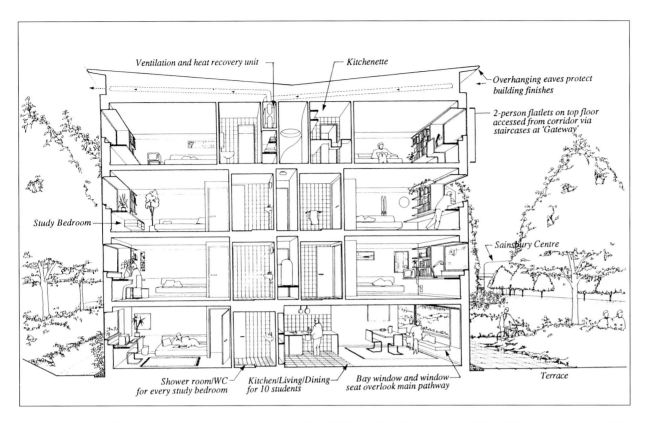

Ventilation and heat recovery unit

Kitchenette

Overhanging eaves protect building finishes

2-person flatlets on top floor accessed from corridor via staircases at 'Gateway'

Study Bedroom

Sainsbury Centre

Shower room/WC for every study bedroom

Kitchen/Living/Dining for 10 students

Bay window and window seat overlook main pathway

Terrace

Constable Terrace and Nelson Court Student Residences (Nelson Court also contains a 'Guest Suite'), by Rick Mather 1991-3, section and plan of unit.

Far right: Drawing of entrance (Rick Mather).

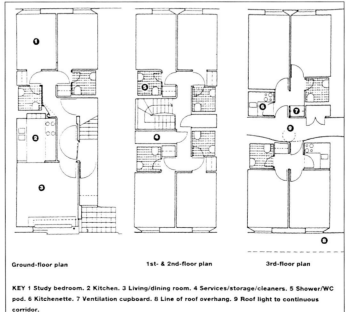

Ground-floor plan

1st- & 2nd-floor plan

3rd-floor plan

KEY 1 Study bedroom. 2 Kitchen. 3 Living/dining room. 4 Services/storage/cleaners. 5 Shower/WC pod. 6 Kitchenette. 7 Ventilation cupboard. 8 Line of roof overhang. 9 Roof light to continuous corridor.

Above: **Nelson Court.**
Below: **Constable Terrace.**

# MATHER'S EARLY POST-MODERNISM IN THE 1980s

'A Lesson in Patronage, Hugh Sockett (top), Tony Evans (left), Gordon Marshall (right), user, clerk of works, and patron'; the School of Education's main staircase, from *the Architect's Journal* 1986.

The University of East Anglia could not complain about a lack of architectural attention during the late 1970s, but British university building as a whole was virtually dead for many years - although the situation at the Seven differed somewhat: Warwick kept building vigorously, while at Kent, Sussex, Lancaster and York the building stock grew modestly; at Essex nothing happened at all. At East Anglia, after an interval of nearly a decade, a number of clever dealings brought new opportunities. In 1981, Keswick Hall (Teacher Training) College was incorporated in the University. The proceeds from the sale of the hall enabled UEA to finance a new building for the School of Education on campus. Another land deal helped to build the Systems School and thus to complete the third wing of the Education School, while a little later Wolfson Foundation money financed the small, separate structure for the successful Climatic Research Unit.

'Development in Norwich has been characterized by the manner in which the leading architectural role - very much that of a master - has passed hand to hand, by personal recommendation', Gillian Darley wrote recently. Certainly, the recommender was a 'master', UEA's consultant architect, Sir Norman Foster. But the same term hardly applied to the recommended, Rick Mather, at the time he began work at UEA. Nor could Mather then have been called an ordinary professional. His was a tiny specialization, the highly sophisticated remodelling of the interior of London terraced houses, including one of the most popular groups of them, the Architectural Association in Bedford Square. In the 1980s Mather continued to build on this fame with a number of sensitive restaurant interiors.

Mather is not given to long theoretical explanations or any kind of rhetoric. He did, however, have something to say about the relationships of his project to Lasdun's buildings: '... you couldn't expect less for this prestigious site ...' In some respects the task was made easier, in that Mather could say that he was going to improve a site which formed a less attractive, indeed, a neglected part of Lasdun's complex. Though Lasdun never intended 'backland spaces', as Mather put it, the area had become drab, mainly through unco-ordinated mass car parking. Mather wanted to provide a protected courtyard and thus created a horseshoe-like building, open to the west, angled at 45 degrees to Lasdun's teaching wall. Mather then thought very hard on further relating his structures to the campus as a whole. He formed the Climatic Research Building like a drum, a 'Temple of the Winds', making it look highly self-contained; at the same time he leads a public passage through it, which is then continued as a path to the Education Building. Mather thus creates some coherent lines of communication on that side of the Teaching Block.

Mather realised that the great mass of Lasdun's Teaching Wall would dominate his modestly-sized three storey building. A difficult task indeed for somebody who had never designed a free-standing building of any size before! But while Mather tried to integrate the grounds, for the Education building itself he went for contrast. The outside appears box-like, without any vertical excrescences. Mather was 'determined to do a building with a facade', in a traditional/post-modern sense of facade as a vertical plane masking the walls, again in total contrast to Lasdun's continuous horizontal bands of concrete and glass. When one says 'facade', 'something that has both large scale register and small detail from close up', the next step is to use the word 'decoration'; indeed, the walls are clad with special surface tiles which also form a number of ornamental bands that do not indicate the structural divisions inside. Part of the fenestration appears as a straightforward, almost simplistic, series of holes in the wall; on the other hand, Mather frequently breaks up the facades with highly irregular groups of openings – again, in defiance of Lasdun's extreme regularity.

The wilfully irregular openings indicate the extraordinary complexity of Mather's interior spaces, which often reach through the whole height of the building - here we get more than an inkling of the skylights of his terraced house conversions. He creates funnel-like vertical openings in the very depth of the building. Mather thus offered something that had been virtually absent from UEA so far: exciting interiors. Lasdun's interiors are the straightforward result of outline, plan and construction; more complex spaces he reserved for the exterior where in places they penetrate several floors. Mather, by contrast, contains the outside of his buildings within box-like or drum-like contours. There was probably a thinking on Lasdun's part that finance simply would not allow any internal spatial 'extras'; indeed, at circa £2.5 m, the costs of Mather's buildings can probably not be called low. The Postmodern sources of his spatial complexities (and the style of architectural drawing that went with it) are to be found in Mather's homeland, the USA: Graves, Venturi, Charles Moore, Robert Stern; a familiar feature is the interpenetration of circles and diagonals, especially at main entrances. Equally varied are Mather's materials. There is little visible reinforced concrete. The interior contrasts forcefully with the exterior, the cheap blockwork facing inside is a conscious continuation of the Feilden period. There is much interior metalwork, too; Mather treats it in a subdued way, rather than in a rhetorical High-Tech manner. His thin metal bridges and perforated steel floors create a 'frisson of unease', in the way they look flimsier than they are. Noting Mather's sense of material, his variation of surface texture and colour one becomes aware, once again, of the changes Post-Modernism had brought; Lasdun's concrete is uniform, solid, 'natural' and goes right through. In retrospect it appears that neither Feilden nor Lasdun ever wanted to use any colour in their constructions. Lastly, no amount of driving rain or sleet can disfigure Mather's exteriors. The 'spectraglaze tiles', new to Britain, were guaranteed against discolouring.

School of Education, main staircase.

Schools of Education and Information Systems,
by Rick Mather 1982-5.

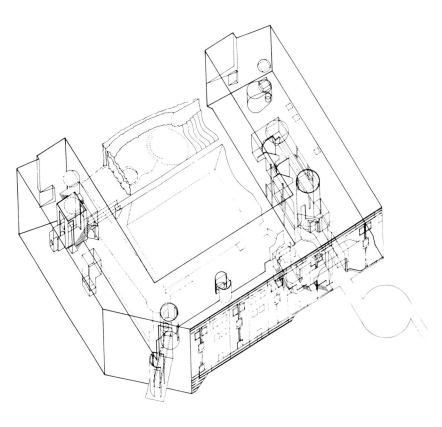

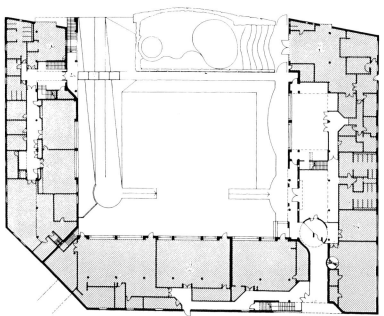

Interior of Systems Building, view of a vertical lightshaft on the third floor.

Climatic Research Unit by Rick Mather, 1984-5.

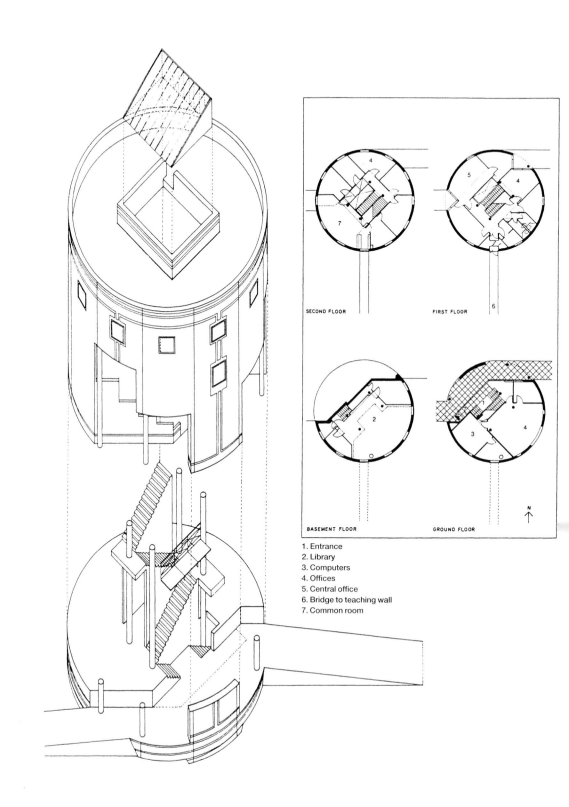

SECOND FLOOR

FIRST FLOOR

BASEMENT FLOOR

GROUND FLOOR

N

1. Entrance
2. Library
3. Computers
4. Offices
5. Central office
6. Bridge to teaching wall
7. Common room

# II NORMAN FOSTER'S SAINSBURY CENTRE

## PATRON AND ARCHITECT, OWNER AND USERS

From Mather we take the longest jump backwards, nearly ten years, to the foundation of the Sainsbury Centre. At this time the local architect Bernard Feilden was in charge of UEA architecture. Feilden watched as the University's most celebrated building went up before his eyes. But he, like everyone else connected with the University, was excluded from contributing to its design, from determining its location. In essence, the project was the work of just two men: The patron, Sir Robert Sainsbury, aided by Lady Lisa Sainsbury, and the architect, Norman Foster, also aided by his wife, Wendy. There was, then, also the Vice-Chancellor, Frank Thistlethwaite's, circumspect handling of the gift on the University's side, and the day-to-day administration of the building process and subsequent general management of the Centre by UEA's Estates Officer, Gordon Marshall. But the chief purpose, the patronage, the style, and the assessment of this building lay outside the normal concerns of the institution and its building activity. There was much comment on the pre-Modern nature of this process of patronage. A later statement by Foster reveals, perhaps unintentionally, the hierarchy of players: 'the building is rooted in the direct working relationship with its patrons, Sir Robert and Lisa Sainsbury, as well as with its owners and users, the UEA'. For Foster, the Sainsburys were 'the toughest and most demanding clients I ever worked for', though he claims... 'we became best friends....'. 'Their own involvement has been

1. The SCVA was officially announced in November 1973, Foster was appointed early 1974; design period 1974-6, building period 1976-7, opening April 1978. – A SCVA Building Committee was established in 1974 (VC, Sainsbury, W.R.Hare (the 'lay' member, in UEA tradition) Prof. A.Martindale head of the School of Fine Arts and Foster. F.Thistlethwaite: 'We ...met rarely... it is fair to say that the effective decisions were taken by Sir Robert and me....'

2. Siting: Foster in 1979: 'The suggestion that the gateway site would help the University's ambivalent relationship with the outside world would be more appropriate if the University was on an urban edge rather than straddling open country and the outer suburban fringes of Norwich.... One of the attractions to the public... is the out-of town rural setting...'. The site

'offers fine views to a new 40 acre lake or broad... framed views... an important component of interior spaces [which] were tested out with models of the interior spaces and back projections, using colour slides taken from the site'. The Landscape Consultant was Lanning Roper.

3. 'Fine Arts' was indeed, a misnomer, there was never any teaching of 'practical art' at UEA, but the choice of the term is indicative of Thistlethwaite's integrative aims. 'Scholarship, and that education through scholarship which is still a university's mission depends on its life and well-being upon words and mathematical symbols... as our culture becomes ever more and more scientific and sociological. And yet, and yet, I have always believed that a liberal education must transcend this means of experience, that it should embrace the expe-

unusually direct and personal at every level.' Sainsbury, on his part, maintained: 'I am very proud that my family name is linked with Norman Foster's building which I regard as aesthetically on a par with the greatest works of art which it houses'. Thistlethwaite's task, by contrast, was merely that of convincing the rest of UEA and the University Grants Committee (UGC) to accept what Sainsbury and Foster had decided and he frankly admits 'that he had to exercise his full authority to get the building through'. [1]

Initially there was the problem of where to place the building. Much consultation and debate took place. A strong faction in the University wanted to site the building near the entrance of the campus in response to the feeling of a lack of contact between city and University and the idea that an attractive 'public building' might help to close the gap. But Foster and Sainsbury rejected this and chose the opposite end of Lasdun's complex, basically because they wanted the best spot in terms of untouched landscape and views. There was, then, no change at this point from the general New University principles of picturesque siting. Foster did, however, construct a slightly more than token link between Lasdun's buildings and the Centre by extending one of Lasdun's walkway platforms with a kind of cat-walk which pierces the skin of his building, like an 'umbilical cord', connecting to the original master architect. The Sainsburys, had, in fact, 'from the beginning... been excited by Sir Denys Lasdun's architecture'. [2]

However much one might be tempted to declare the Sainsbury Centre a seminal building which just happens to be located within UEA grounds, its links with the University should not be neglected. The Centre does not just mean the building and the collection but it also contains an 'institution', and quite a complex one at that, and in this respect it was shaped at least in some measure by the 'owner and user', to quote again Foster's order of the players. Many of the day to day users, did, indeed, feel they were the last to be asked, even bypassed, in spite of an elaborate process of consultation. The first contacts between UEA and the Sainsburys were made by Frank Thistlethwaite and they date back almost to the origin of the University. The visual arts had always been a strong element in Thistlethwaite's thinking about education. With the initial encouragement of the Sainsburys and with the assistance of the art historians at

Searching for the site: From left: Gordon Marshall, UEA Estates Officer, Sir Robert Sainsbury, Lady Sainsbury and Norman Foster (c. 1974).

rience of the fine arts. This is a dimension of education which the universities have never fully absorbed into their tradition.'

4. The term Arts Centre (not normally used for the SCVA) brings to mind the near contemporary Gardner Arts Centre at Sussex University of 1967-70 or the Arts Centre at Warwick University. These, however, include also the performing arts and the spaces devoted to art collections or art exhibitions are relatively small. The SCVA is thus much larger than most University Art Galleries'. Frank Thistlethwaite's boastful: '... Ashmole at Oxford, Fitzwilliam at Cambridge, Courtauld in London... and now ...', may sound somewhat inappropriate at first, but with regard to the size of building the comparison appears not too far fetched.

An initial stipulation that children were not allowed in the gallery was fairly soon rescinded. Sainsbury on the planning of the interior (after receiving briefs for the Senior Common Room and for the School of Fine Arts, i.e. the Art History Sector, 'there would be no written brief for the Sainsbury accommodation within the centre'. Foster's principal philosophy was that the building should be flexible and evolutionary. Peter Yorke (2000): 'I wrote these briefs... in our traditional Estate Office terms, which Foster thought outdated. That was the main reason why he agreed to accept them only as a guide'.

5. Mies van der Rohe's Neue Nationalgalerie in Berlin and the Louisiana Museum for modern art in Denmark impressed them most. The Sainsburys' selections of works had not been

UEA, Alastair Grieve and Peter Lasko, the VC, embarked on a small collection of strictly Modernist, that is abstract and Constructivist art, to form the 'University Art Collection', which was to maintain a semi independent existence from the Sainsbury Gift. As early as 1969 a separate 'Fine Arts Building' was conceived to house the collection and the Art History Sector of the School of Fine Arts and Music. Soon in fact, the Music Sector of that School obtained its own building. On the occasion of the opening of the Sainsbury Centre the Vice Chancellor stressed again his concept of a 'liberal education... which should embrace the experience of the Fine Arts...'. Frank Thistlethwaite had become friends with the Sainsburys and, as he recalls, 'we talked, off and on, about them lending the University some pictures. However, this idea hung fire for a while because we did not have the money for a suitable building...' Then, in May 1973 Robert and Lisa Sainsbury proposed to Thistlethwaite that they would give their entire collection to the University; in addition, David Sainsbury provided the finance for a new building to house it. [3]

There was throughout a stress on the informal and 'private' nature of the whole undertaking, both in the way the collection had come about in the first place, and in the way it was now to be newly used by the University. The Sainsburys principal aim had been to serve their private enjoyment. In donating the collection to the University, the idea was that young women and men should also live with it in a 'domestic' way - the main gallery space was to be called 'the Living Area' - and that it should form a part of the grain and texture of University life. 'We want to give some men and some women - and who better than undergraduates in a school of fine arts? - the opportunity of looking at works of art in the natural context of their work and daily life...' The Sainsburys hoped that the students would enjoy the art from an aesthetic and not only an intellectual aspect, because sensual response was the basis upon which they themselves had been collecting. Furthermore, they felt - when asked 'why UEA?' - that 'a new university clearly lends itself to our project in a way not possible at the older universities'.

It was at first envisaged that the public would only be admitted in small numbers. However, with the incorporation of numerous facilities for the general public, and in particular a restaurant and café

made to construct a particular thesis about art. Sir Robert said, 'I have never regarded myself as a collector in the most usually accepted sense of the word - that is to say, I have always refused to acquire something merely because it filled a gap, or added to the representation of a particular art form... I have, for over 40 years, been a passionate acquirer of works of art that have appealed to me, irrespective of period or style ...' The accumulation is thus exceptionally broadly based, with African, Oceanic, North American and Middle and South American, Asian, European and Middle Eastern artifacts as well as 19th – 20th-cent-ury European drawings, paintings and sculptures. Much of the work is figurative, and many objects are quite small. By the time of the opening of the SCVA there were about 700 objects.

6. Foster's own approach in the planning of large buildings neatly corresponded at this point to the Sainsburys' intentions. He begins with: 'There was an obvious distaste for monuments' Foster normally made few remarks about any general 'social' qualities of his buildings, however, a much quoted comment about his Willis Faber Building in Ipswich ran: '... technology no longer seen as an end in itself but as directed towards achieving social goals ...'; hence the 'umbrella form of this building being rooted in the avoidance of 'we and they', the management box and workers' shed', 'posh and scruffy', 'clean and dirty', 'back and front.'

Norman Foster: The idea of the 'skin' excited the team of architects and engineers (the latter led by Tony Hunt) , but it made them nervous. They were a long way down one design path and to propose another change when Sir Robert was clearly happy with the existing

such limited access would not have made sense, indeed it would have appeared ill-advised, conceived as it was, during the 1970s, in a period in which the University's reputation in Norwich and the region was low. Once it was open, there was never any doubt of the Centre's main function as a public art gallery. Thistlethwaite was keen to see the building open to all, as 'not just a stuffy gallery but an important social centre for the university.'[4]

There was 'no brief' for the building – a phrase, as we shall see, with a familiar ring at UEA. A long process of design followed. One further element which had prompted the gift was the fact that the Sainsburys had just seen their collection on show in its entirety at the Kroeller-Muller Museum in Holland. It was the first time their art works had been properly displayed. This event also determined the choice of the designer, the Dutch-Indonesian architect Kho Liang Ie (much praised for the interior of Amsterdam's Schiphol Airport), for the interior layout. Unfortunately, a few months later he died of cancer. By this time, Norman Foster had been appointed as the exterior architect (after the Sainsburys had seen his building for the Olsen Centre at London Docks) and it was now agreed he should take on the entire project, while much of the actual display design and the screens were, and still are, undertaken by the American designer George Sexton. The Sainsburys and the Fosters then made an intensive tour of new galleries and museums in Europe, which, however, did not provide them with any direct models. In fact, Kho Liang Ie's model continued to influence the layout of the exhibits. He had impressed the Sainsburys with his 'reinvention' of the art exhibition. He took the art off the walls and displayed it free-standing. Thus rather than walking around a room following the chronology of paintings and sculptures, the viewer is offered a landscape of paintings and sculptures divided by temporary partitions. Such an approach is eminently suitable for a disparate collection that is not chronological or themed but depends rather on sensual coherence. The 'landscape approach' - where you look across spaces and see a number of aesthetically related objects and pictures in one glance – has remained the hallmark of the Sainsbury Centre display.[5]

Brief or no brief, the programme soon grew more and more complex, largely because of the incor-

Sir Henry Moore discusses the placing of one of his reclining figures. From left to right: Michael Paulson-Ellis Registrar, Prof. John Fletcher, Sir Henry Moore, Sir Robert Sainsbury, Norman Foster.

design was bound to cause an almighty row. Would the Sainsburys' good will evaporate? Tony Hunt agreed that Foster's new idea was a better design, but pragmatically he suggested completing the building to its existing design and saving the new ideas for a future project. Wendy, a partner in the firm, said, 'No!' After hours of debate the new design was agreed and was also committed to the same budget and the same schedule – Foster dared not do anything else. The initial reaction of the Sainsburys to the proposed change of design was disbelief. Foster remembers:'...How could we propose yet more changes just when everyone had grown accustomed to a scheme which had been finally approved? I urged them to consider it on its merits: after all, had they, too, not been responsible for changes during the evolution of the project? Had we not jointly agreed at the outset to achieve the best possible building within the

allotted time and cost?' After further intensive discussion all parties agreed to the design.

Another major design struggle occurred over the idea to continue the University Walkway through the first floor of the 'skin' of the building, alongside, but independently of the main gallery, in order to provide a direct connection with the restaurant and public facilities beyond; this was not allowed for reasons of fire protection.

A mid-1975 account of the building makes interesting reading: 'A large tube, internally white, externally reflective... glass panels... sometimes on the side, sometimes above... big adjustable louvres... not only make it easier to show art objects but a nice place to be... enjoying the ever-changing English skies... Inside, full height glass divisions happen across the tube to allow control of different environments... whilst maintaining visual contact and awareness.

The old external skin.

poration of the art history teaching facilities. The possibility of grouping four or five buildings together, each with its own function, was considered and quickly rejected. From the very earliest discussions, Foster was intrigued by the elegance of the idea of throwing a single roof over everything - one grand architectural gesture in the spirit of an engineer who apparently casually flings a bridge across a gorge. But behind the scenes in Foster's office the architects were struggling with the detailed planning. Their vision of open galleries and long interior views was disturbed by utilitarian 'lumps' which kept intruding into the central spaces - boilers, mechanical equipment and lavatories. Late in the day, a solution suggested itself. Why not give the building a double skin, with sufficient space between the exterior and interior walls to house services such as heating and ventilation, lavatories, photographic darkrooms and storerooms, thus leaving the primary spaces free and uncluttered? After some toing and froing the patron finally agreed with the architect. [6]

## CRITIQUES, NATIONAL AND LOCAL

At the end of the account of Lasdun's architecture it will be noted that no proper critical architectural assessment of his campus ever occurred. There were pictorial and technical accounts and there were plenty of quotations from Lasdun's own rhetorical descriptions. This lack of assessment was due, mainly, to the fact that Lasdun's campus was never 'completed', or at least, never formally opened, and, secondly, it was due to the way in which, by 1969-70, its architecture had already begun to go out of fashion; indeed, the one careful analysis of Lasdun's UEA which belatedly followed in 1972 was largely negative. Lasdun's greatest 'critical' days, so to speak, had occurred at the very beginning, with the great models of 1963. With the Sainsbury Centre the opposite was to happen: very little attention, almost secrecy in the early stage, and a blaze of publicity at the opening in April 1978. Critics literally descended upon the building, not only those directly from the professional journals, but all kinds of fel-

---

...The building is open-ended, never finished but complete at any stage.'

The exact costs of the undertaking were never accurately disclosed: '....costs: confidential'. 'Original estimate £1.9m, actual cost £2.5 m' (June 1977). Sainsbury's original endowment (given by David Sainsbury, Sir Robert's son) was £ 3.7m, which included money for the future additions to the collection. The total cost of the building by April 1978 was £3.7m. The UGC gave £ 600.000 to pay for the faculty and teaching accommodation, as well as for catering spaces - all designed according to UGC norms. However, inflation led to David Sainsbury's donating a further half million pounds to the building project and to his agreeing that of the one and a half million pounds originally earmarked for art purchases, some £ 450 000 could be spent on the building.

7. Rogers continued: 'The glistening gray interior space is dynamic, spartan and spare; flexibility and enclosure are reconciled in the precise yet fluid machine environment. The lightweight all-enclosing zipped/unzipped skin wraps around Tony Hunt's brilliant semi-exposed skeletal structure which contains the mechanical services. There are always concepts that we might question and challenge, but I prefer to recognise that this is a uniquely audacious and heroic statement carried out with perfect control. It offers food for thought and gives true delight.'

Maxwell continues his comparison of the SCVA with the Parthenon: 'One is a CELLA, the other is a SHED, but both are strictly rational and fully frontal, with a portico attached at either end, one of which is clearly marked 'front' and the other 'back'.

low practitioners, academics and theorists as well. Their disourses, which they partly conducted amongst themselves, were much more broadly based than any of those provoked by Lasdun. There was no question of simply citing the architect's or the patron's intentions. In any case, compared with Lasdun's 'romantic language' (Lasdun), Foster's was restrained; the purpose of his comments was always the detailed explanation of plan and construction, much of it highly technical, and there is little of rhetoric and metaphors in his speech. It was now that the critics vied with each other in their praise, and often their language was elevated indeed.

No less than twenty professionals were asked to comment by *Architectural Design*. Richard Rogers, Foster's erstwhile partner, began: 'Let us not be mealy-mouthed. By dint of sweat, imagination and superb control Norman Foster has produced two superb buildings [SCVA and the Willis Faber Dumas Offices in Ipswich] which stand proudly and lonely amongst the mediocrity that surrounds us'. '…An elegant solution of creating a modern temple for art, teaching and the public… A shimmering changing light gives an ethereal steely substance to the interior.' Robert Maxwell, one of the most noted architectural commentators and defenders of Modernism, began his short piece with: 'The year of the Sainsbury Centre, as it happens, was the year I finally saw the Parthenon: both experiences were exhilarating. The comparison is far fetched but not entirely pointless …'. Others took a more historical line: 'A typical Late-Modern building' (Charles Jencks); 'it comes in the tradition of the Miesian attempt to create the "Well-Serviced Shed"' (Ron Herron); it is something that 'Leonidov dreamt of' (David Wild). [7]

Predictably, there was some left-wing criticism, for instance in the most extensive account of all, carried in the same issue of *Architectural Design* in early 1979, by Andrew Peckham, himself more an academic than a critic. His analysis, in its density somewhat reminiscent of the criticism of Essex University of the early 1970s, takes on the 'ideology' of the institution and the building. Peckham was alerted to the 'undemocratic' way in which the Centre had been commissioned, and was doubtful about its social purposes and sceptical of the merits of the collection. [8]

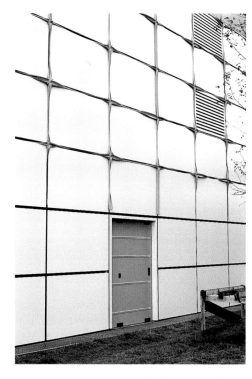

The new external skin being fitted, 1988.

8. More on the poetic side is John Maule McKean, writing in a style that seems arch even for an architectural critic and particularly so when compared to his sober analytical account of Essex University in the *Architects' Journal* of 1972. '… But then it's dark. Bitter cold, driving sleet and snow as I walk the long narrow high bridge from the little town of Lasdun et al, towards the lighted hole, high in that huge gray shadow. The glass airlock swings open. Silver and gray, mist and sparkle into space. The soft warm purring mechanical inside, vast as the eye can see… the science fiction hive… the secret space station… the underground city… But here, somehow, it's theatrically friendly; an intimate hugeness; spacious to take the different pursuits, but as among the "living area" burolandschaft - small; and Superman's tiny crystalline lift all at home within its shimmering louvered aluminum tent and reflective gables. I wonder what the Crystal Palace was like at night?'

Peckham: 'The neutral display of the collection does invite comparison with the nineteenth-century exhibitions equating culture with information… a phantasmagoria of capitalist culture'. 'Foster's reductionist aesthetic, presenting an image of accessible culture - a supermarket or sports centre - does mirror the collection'… 'relegation of the significance of art to a neutral aesthetic experience… indeed is consistent with the deliberate contradiction of offering such a collection to an art history department rather than an art school.' Further headings of the contributions in *Architectural Design*: 'A Critique of the Sainsbury Centre'. 'This is the Modern World'. 'The Collection'. 'The Location'. 'The Building as Object (Form)'. 'The Building as Servicing Mechanism (Technology)'. 'The Building as Content (Social Role and Organsiation)'.

But there was a quite different kind of criticism which did not come with the stylish language of the professional critic, but from inside the building. It came, so to speak, from below the elevated level of the patron and the architect. This was the voice of some of the permanent users of the building. It was usually prefaced by a full acknowledgment of the superb visual qualities and the stylistic novelty of Foster's work, but it then stressed that those values appeared completely divorced from the problems of the daily use of the building. Faculty members of the School of Fine Arts (i.e. the art historians) pointed to 'certain serious defects in the design of the building which they would like to bring to the notice of the Senate', as it was termed in the first Report, of November 1977. The chief complaint was the 'utter inadequacy of the sound insulation' of the lecturer's offices, which were also to be their teaching rooms. A year later a survey was undertaken by the School. 87 % of staff and students surveyed found that noise levels in the new rooms were higher than in Arts Block I, the previous home of the School. It was also pointed out that the architect had been notified many times of these problems, but appeared not to have done very much about it. Some sound insulation was subsequently fitted. The second most common complaint was about the problems of lecturing in the building; after some delays an adequate lecture room was installed in the basement. Third in severity was the way in which users of the offices had to bend down to unlock the doors, as the locks are embedded into the floor. They still have to bend down. Back troubles, which were feared to be the result have not so far manifested themselves. [9]

In another respect Foster's ideas were completely vindicated; complaints about the openness of the School's area soon died down. Finally, there is the most serious general problem concerning the interior of the Centre: air conditioning. It usually comes as a surprise to visitors when they are told that the building is not air conditioned, in the sense that, although mechanically ventilated and heated, the interior is not artificially cooled. The temperature on a hot summer's day can reach into the nineties Fahrenheit (up to 35 degrees centigrade). On the other hand, heating the vast space is said to be comparatively expensive. [10]

9. Somewhat later Prof. Andrew Martindale expressed the lecturer's concerns in an even more strongly worded letter. There was a general sense that, in spite of the claims of flexibility, the metal building was inherently inflexible. A sharply Marxist and profoundly critical analysis of the institution was circulated informally at a History Workshop Meeting (undated, c.1980, probably written by art history lecturer Nicholas Green). Yet another criticism, voiced by the staff and lecturer's union was concerned with the expense of the opening events and the threat of heavy running costs generally.

As regards the lecturers' rooms: it must be recalled that the design and grouping of these rooms had gone through a long process; early on Foster had proposed freely movable cubicles, open at the top; this was ruled out by the lecturers on grounds of lack of privacy. Foster had a hard task with the art history faculty because in their first home in the University Village they had enjoyed a great deal of fresh air and views over grass and trees they were then placed into the darkish lowest floor of Lasdun's teaching block, which, however, still provided a fair amount of daylight. Understandably there was now discontent about the darkness of their rooms under the mezzanine floor in the SCVA. Opinions about the open court for the general use of the school were mostly positive from the start. Foster's promise to eliminate dark corridors seemed amply fulfilled. In Sainsbury's later words: Foster is 'always ready to change his mind... ready to listen to the opinions of others however humble the individuals may be.'

All this criticism, in turn, was evaluated in several ways. First of all, it was too strong to remain a purely internal matter, not least because of the architect's frequent claim that he genuinely cares for the users' every practical concern. The problems were still alluded to by Martin Pawley in one of his 'Building Revisits' in 1984 and by Foster himself in 1985. There was, however, another angle to be taken in all this: the mundane complaints of some of the users appeared as one side of a local - national polarisation, of the gap between metropolitan professional / artistic progress and provincial backwardness, an issue that had come to prominence already under Lasdun. Peter Cook, in what was probably the most stylish and the most incisive of all the contemporary critiques of the Sainsbury Centre, conjures up an attack by Foster on both 'tweedy provincialism' and 'technical mediocrity... the architectural Jeremiahs who will gleefully remind you of your drips, splinterings and sweatings (of which this building has a couple). They will suggest that a more humane or gentle (they mean timid) building would have "breathed" more easily'. He could well at that point have referred to Bernard Feilden, who continued to disapprove of the building. Furthermore, according to Cook, 'the academics of such places are notoriously opinionated and neurotic'. There was even a kind of assessment that could mean both criticism and praise, namely with the 'High Tech' metaphors such as 'hangar' or 'Hindenburg airship'. For technology fans of the 1970s this meant pure praise and excitement, for others it meant a reluctant coming to terms with the strangeness of the building.

In the end, it did not seem to be in the interest of the University to sustain its criticism. The art historians knew only too well from their study of the tradtional patronage of great buildings that posterity would simply sweep away their seemingly insignificant complaints. The Collection and the exhibition space have provided UEA with a foothold in the international museum-world, while there is no question that there are local benefits, too. As far as Foster's great 'shed', or 'temple' is concerned, the biggest compliment is probably paid by those, who, a quarter of century on, still come to see it as if it was a new building.

10. Air conditioning: In 1975 we read: 'The combination of the generous internal height, opening panels and reflective cladding are all devices to obtain comfort conditions without resorting to the expense and high energy input of air conditioning'. The contradictions in Foster's approach to these problems were already discussed in 1972: 'Ecologists criticise Foster's Buildings for their high energy technological input ...'. Foster tried to extricate himself variously by pointing to the high insulation value of the 'skin', or by saying that the 'absence of air conditioning is also in the spirit of a living room environment, rather than a climate controlled vault for works of art'. Martin Pawley believed that air conditioning could be put in at any time. One major reason for its absence, however, appears that it would require ventilators of a colossal size to change the warm air in the centre into cool air.

In 1978 Foster was made Consultant Architect to UEA. The outgoing Consultant, Feilden, had specified that his successor must be of 'international standing'.

Foster in 2000: The issue of temperature control in the Centre. It is not true to say that the building cannot be air-conditioned. It certainly could, but during the design process, in discussion with both the University and the Sainsburys, it was felt that the considerable first and running costs of air-conditioning did not merit their installation when the mechanical ventilation and the heat stack effect of the lofty interior would cope with most days of an English summer. The design direction taken was responsible and energy conscious at a time when such matters were not often discussed.

Left above: **The elevated walkway. Later view with passage leading into the Crescent Wing. Reclining Figure by Henry Moore (1956-62).**
Left below: **The elevated walkway.**

**Right: Early air view of the Sainsbury Centre.**

## THE SAINSBURY CENTRE FOR THE VISUAL ARTS

Norman Foster 1977/8: 'The close physical proximity of activities (galleries are usually confined to viewing and schools to teaching) offers the benefit of cross fertilization in the spirit of the original brief. For the Gallery the chief aims were: the positive qualities of tuneable top lighting (in the roof zone) and the need to service the gallery without disturbing either exhibits or users. The structure is of welded steel tube (Engineers: Anthony Hunt Associates), freely expressed at the ends. The inner skin or lining consists of perforated aluminum louvres, those under the ceiling are adjustable from a computerized console. There are additional banks of louvres under the glazed areas at the top. The external panels are like 'sandwiches': foam-filled with a moulded outer skin of superplastic anodised aluminium, interchangeable by merely undoing six bolts. A basement in poured concrete runs underneath the length of the building'.

Foster greatly developed the new 1960s trend of having building components factory produced, especially in the case of the external panels, here obtained from TI Superform Ltd. of Tube Investments Ltd. The joints between them were fitted with a 'lattice work of extruded neoprene rubber' by BTR subsidiary Leyland and Birmingham Rubber Co. Both elements were novelties, as regards production and application. From an overall view of structure and form it was claimed that we witness for the first time a building in which walls and roofs are covered by the same device. Inside, the louvres, as such, were common-place products, but their use as 'walls' was novel. Again, the same product is used for the walls and the ceiling. There is then the more general assessment of a High Tech style. Most of these factors make of Foster's building one of the pioneers of extreme High Tech, in the sense of the rejection of conventional building materials and constructional practice. On the other hand, Foster does not participate in a specific version of High Tech which not only searches for novelty in frame and walls, but, influenced by the Archigram movement of the 1960s, emphasizes the service functions, such as pipework, stairs, lifts and by literally turning the building inside-out makes these elements ultra visible. The Sainsbury Centre thus differs strongly from the Pompidou Centre in Paris which went up during the same years. For Foster, at least with the Sainsbury Centre, the 'extraneous, but necessary rooms and equipment' should be hidden 'in search for the perfect skin and architectural idiom pared down to the absolute minimum'. - The Centre was built on a management contract, with Bovis as Building Adviser to Carter as Management Contractor.

By 1987 so many of the external panels were defective (water vapour penetrated through hairline cracks to the foam which created a liquid which corroded the panels) that they had to be replaced by plastic-coated steel panels.

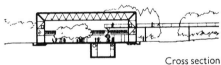

Cross section

### Dimensions

| | |
|---|---|
| External length | 131.4 m |
| Internal length | 122.4 m |
| External width | 35.0 m |
| Internal width | 29.0 m |
| External height | 10.3 m |
| Internal height | 7.3 m |
| Ground floor area | 3550.0 m² |
| Mezzanine floor area | 835.0 m² |
| Basement floor area | 1066.0 m² |
| Service core area | 735.0 m² |
| Total area | 6186.0 m² |

### Sainsbury Centre ground floor

1 Terrace
2 Restaurant
3 Kitchen
4 School of fine arts
5 Study reserve
6 Living area/gallery
7 Conservatory
8 Coffee bar
9 Special exhibition area
10 Sculpture terrace
11 Service wall
12 High level link to rest of university
13 Ground level entrance

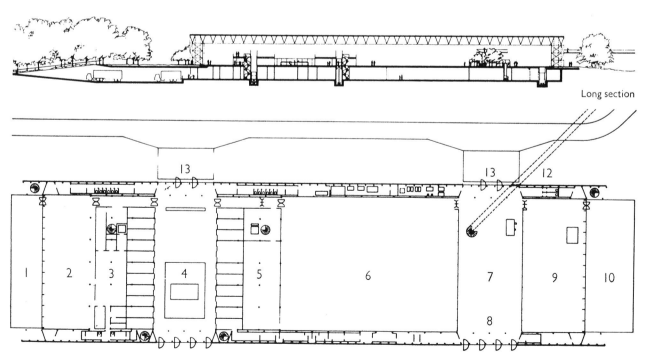

Long section

Below: **Construction c. 1976.**

Following pages:
P. 40: **Catwalk in the roof, photograph by Ken Kirkwood at the beginning of the** *Architectural Design* **Special Issue of 1979.**
P. 41: **West elevation**

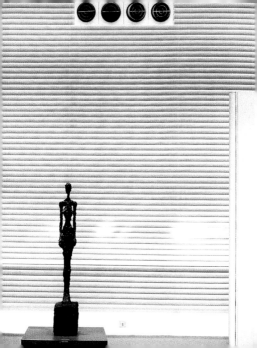

Above: Gallery towards East.
Below: Gallery towards West with Sir Robert Sainsbury and the first Gallery Keeper, Alan Borg.

Above: The Restaurant Area.
Below: The 'School' Area (School of World Art Studies and Museology Art History Sector, formerly School of Fine Arts) and the former Senior Common Room on the Mezzanine.

## THE SAINSBURY CENTRE CRESCENT WING 1989-1991.

An extension of the Sainsbury gift, it enlarges the area of the original Sainsbury Centre by almost half. The building had become necessary partly through omissions in the first structure, partly through the growth of the collection and the new developments in conservation and other branches of museum technology. At first a lengthening of the main building was considered - acting upon the principle that the 'shed' was infinitely extendable, but to the Sainsburys the building was 'a finite object, perfect in itself'. The underground solution then suggested itself as a continuation of the Centre's large concrete basement and by the slope on the Eastern side of the main structure. The extension contains a multitude of functions: A large lecture-cum exhibition room suitable for all those objects which cannot be exposed to daylight; ample room for the 'Study Collection' and for conservation, storage, for curatorial and other offices, the latter now receive (almost) direct daylight. A great deal more care was spent on the methods of exhibiting and especially lighting, artificial as well natural (Lighting Consultant: George Sexton).

Right: The corridor of the Crescent Wing; offices of the Curators, the Museology Section and the Sainsbury Research Unit for the Arts of Africa. Oceania and the Americas (SRU).

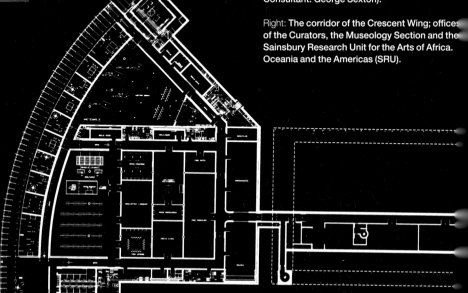

# III  UEA 1962 - 1974
# The Campus of Denys Lasdun and Frank Thistlethwaite

## THE SEARCH FOR AN ARCHITECT

One of the chief characteristics of the foundation process of the Seven New Universities was the way in which the architectural concept was seen to be part and parcel of the institutional and academic concept. For UEA, it might be argued that the choice of the principal architect was altogether the institution's greatest coup, at least in its early years. But the process of choosing the designer could be fraught with problems, as British universities excluded a method of selection which in such cases provides a fair, but also a cumbersome procedure, namely the competition.

How did UEA have such foresight in 1961? In actual fact, Lasdun had not been the University's first choice. In 1959 the local UEA Promotion Committee (for UEA's early history turn to page 135) was receiving unsolicited inquiries from local architects, but its secretary, Gordon Tilsley, stressed that the University was to be an undertaking with an 'international reputation, [and] therefore the architecture had to be the best that could be procured.' Timothy Colman, promoter of the Appeal Fund, recommended: '... go national, even international in the choice of the architect; the appeal [will be] favourably affected if we are able to have a renowned architect'. In April 1961 Tilsley visited Guy Oddie, an architect working at the University Grants Committee, who first of all told him that the UGC's advice had to remain informal; he then stressed: avoid practitioners who 'produce flashy perspectives'; choose one who had a sound organization behind him because all detailed work was done by junior staff members.' Oddie was then pressed by Tilsley to comment upon a number of names. What of Professor Sir Leslie Martin at Cambridge? Oddie thought him a step ahead of public taste but this did not mean his buildings were necessarily worthwhile; Chamberlin, Powell and Bon were held to be suitable coordinating architects. For himself Oddie would choose a good local-authority architect. Dame Evelyn Sharp, of the Ministry of Housing and Local Government, recommended Philip Dowson, Chamberlin, Powell and Bon, but not top designers such as Sir Basil Spence because they were too busy with other commissions. [1]

UEA turned to Martin. A site meeting with him on July 8 1961 was attended by Lord Mackintosh, the Chairman of the Promotion / Executive Committee, and Gordon Tilsley. No Vice-chancellor had yet been appointed. Martin showed himself enthusiastic about the site. Discussion soon turned to a point that was to be the crux of much of the role of the architect at UEA. Martin freely admitted that he did not have a large organization behind him, and that it would be necessary for him to employ a team of associate architects. However, he would endeavour to produce a large flexible plan, undertake one or two of the principal buildings himself, and then lay down the pattern to which the associates would design. But Lord Mackintosh said 'he would like there to be one mind and one style throughout the University building', and he was concerned that this consistency of style would be lost if too many people had a hand in the work. Mackintosh was perhaps not entirely aware of the way in which he was the first to state the most important maxim of UEA's architecture and patronage. Martin readily agreed, stressing that the associate architects would need firm direction. Viscount Cranbrook then stepped in to play Devil's advocate and asked what would happen if this single voice and firm direction became too strong. Surely it would prevent a succeeding generation from creating its own style? Martin recovered his composure quickly and said that a great deal of the layout must remain 'easy and informal'. In the end, another argument came to the fore: some full-time practising architects felt a grievance that academic architects like Martin were taking work from them. By September Martin felt it necessary to withdraw. [2]

By now the University had a Vice-Chancellor. Frank Thistlethwaite was keenly interested in art and Modernist architecture. Cambridge was in those years a hotbed of advanced architectural projects. In his own College, St. John's, Thistlethwaite was involved with a competition for the Cripps building. One of the chief competitors was Lasdun (see the precedents for the Ziggurats below), who was also just building one of the largest new colleges, Fitzwilliam. In addition, Lasdun received some criticism with his tower block proposals for the Cambridge Science Laboratories. There was, in addition, Sir Charles Wilson, the Chairman of the Norwich Academic Planning Board, who, as Vice-Chancellor at Leicester,

1. Initially Martin was recommended by Sir John Cockcroft, of the new Churchill College Cambridge. Martin appeared matter of fact on all issues of administration, economy, research, fees. Martin to Tilsley: 1. Martin would help the University draw up schedules of accommodation and then work these into specific buildings with the object of producing a master plan to show the layout of the whole site. 2. At the same time he would study technical solutions, enabling buildings to be economically and rapidly constructed. 3. The master plan would help to devise schedules for timing the building work. At this stage a team of associates would be brought into help.

2. Letter from Timothy Colman to Frank Thistlethwaite, end of October 1961:
'Architects:... It is not in my province to promote any one name in this matter and, indeed, I am afraid I know very little about the recent works of individual architects.... When the matter was first mentioned some months ago, however, I did make one or two enquiries privately and for what they are worth I forward them to you, asking that you should use them with discretion as I don't wish to be sued for libel! 1) Sir William Holford - First class. 2) Yorke, Rosenberg & Mardall - designed, I believe, the much-praised airport at Gatwick. 3) Collins, Melvin Ward - Castrol House in Marylebone Road. 4) Matthew & Johnson-Marshall - building New Zealand House in the Haymarket? 5) Llewellyn Davis - Has recently undertaken extensions to Tate Gallery. Would it be worth considering anyone from abroad or is this too dashing? 6) Oscar Niemeyer - Designed most of the buildings in Brasilia. Has a "plastic" technique. 7) Mies vander Roke [sic] - Designed many buildings in New York and has great following in U.S. 8) Gio Ponti - Has built the Pirelli

had commissioned Lasdun with a hostel and the University Social Centre. Apparently Martin was also recommending Lasdun. Opinions were gathered, most notably from the then RIBA President, Sir William Holford (soon himself to be designated as architect at Kent). He was quite positive, but warned that Lasdun was a man 'who likes to carry out all his designs...'. However, by January 1962 it appeared certain that Lasdun was to be UEA's designer [3]

## AN ARCHITECT-CLIENT RELATIONSHIP 1962-68

One is tempted to call Lasdun the Grand Old Man of English Modernist architecture. Undoubtedly, during most of the 1960s and 1970s Lasdun and Stirling were the most respected figures of the architectural establishment. However, Lasdun, being somewhat older, did not quite keep up with innovations, and thus by the 1980s, the triumvirate was named as Stirling, Foster and Rogers. In late 1961, when UEA approached Lasdun, the situation was rather different. Although Lasdun had been designing buildings, even large complexes, for nearly twenty five years, he was, by then, only five or so years into what he himself considered his mature phase, and was only then completing his first building of seminal importance, the Royal College of Physicians in Regents Park. After that, however, important projects mushroomed, to name only the first proposal for the National Theatre and Opera House, in 1965. In addition, Lasdun's numerous buildings and competition designs for Cambridge were gaining him nationwide fame and also controversial attention. Strictly speaking, at UEA, one should not talk just of Lasdun, but of 'Lasdun and his team', within which individual members were given a fair degree of independence.

Yet it is one thing to discuss the design ideals of New University architecture and present a photogenic and rhetorical account of a grand design; there is quite another story to be told about the actual design and construction process. From a mundane viewpoint a university is a huge complex which contains upwards of 2000 rooms for a multitude of activities around an elaborate communication system.

Tower in Milan. I think perhaps it might be too controversial to risk going abroad and might also take too much time at this stage. Do not hesitate to ignore all these suggestions which are merely names.'

3. UEA began to debate Lasdun, it appears, in late October 1961; by then Thistlethwaite had already visited him. On November 3 1961, Lasdun wrote to him expressing enthusiasm; a site meeting was held on November 22 1961. Gordon Tilsley (1996) about a visit to Lasdun's office: 'We were shown photographs of Lasdun's Bethnal Green Housing Block and of the College of ...?... [Royal College of Physicians]; we approved Lasdun'.

Holford on November 29 1961 to Mackintosh: He (Holford) had tried to get Martin to change his mind but failed and then added, 'we all have great confidence in his nominee, Denys Lasdun. He is, however, a man who likes to carry out all his designs and we have very little experience of him in the role of consulting architect and planner.' 'But to take complete charge over the first five year period of construction I could suggest (in addition to Denys Lasdun) a number of other firms such as James Cubitt and Partners, or Yorke, Rosenberg and Mardall ...'. On December 1 1961 FT told Lasdun that the Academic Planning Board would approve and that no difficulties were expected from the Executive Committee (the Governing Body of the University).

4. York and East Anglia: government approval in April 1960; architects appointed: York April 1961, UEA (officially) March 1962; York: Development plan May 1962, East Anglia 'Draft I' i

with some added and very specialized service mechanisms for the sciences. There was no clear definition of the university as a client; or, rather, more often than not it was unclear as to 'who is able to, or empowered to speak on behalf of the institution as a client' (Peter Yorke). The eventual client of such an undertaking consists of a conglomerate of diverse individuals, teachers, researchers, librarians, caterers and many more and their predictions of the functioning of their buildings. Initially, however, at the stage of formulating the general layout, there was usually the closest co-operation of a very small number of people, the architect and his partners, prominent members of the 'lay' Council and one or two officers of the university, but above all the vice-chancellor. None of the Seven can be taken as typical in the way it went about the architect-client relationship. At York it was at its most disciplined, at Essex probably at its most intense; at Sussex there were some difficulties in dealing with a prima donna architect, while late Lancaster seemed to be a reasonably smooth process. Kent's and Warwick's initial severe planning hiccups no longer really mattered when, very swiftly, the first phase of the complex had been completed. At East Anglia, the process was seemingly at its most complex, but it contained elements of most of the others. There was the usual uncompromising stress on 'the whole' but the actual process of briefing could probably be called more democratic at UEA than elsewhere, at least in intention, as the architect was meant to be answerable to a number of committees. In 1968 Thistlethwaite briefly referred to the self-governing Oxbridge tradition and its 'aim of a high degree of self-deliberative discussion'. In practice, however, in an undertaking that arose out of nothing, the vice-chancellor's role was as vital as at York or Essex. In any case, UEA was the slowest of the Seven. The architect had made his decision by very late 1961, but the first buildings were taken into use only in late 1966. What took nearly five years at UEA most of the other seven achieved in little over three years. At UEA difficulties were the order of the day, caused by the architect's high-handedeness, by the client's indecision, and by the UGC's continuous tightening of the purse-strings. [4, 8]

Nobody, of course, could have foreseen that actual story at UEA at that point. But the trouble had begun even before the beginning, so to speak: Lasdun's official appointment was delayed by two months because of a dispute over the level of fees. Mackintosh tried to set UGC fees, but Lasdun wanted RIBA fees. Lasdun said there had to be a considerable degree of trust between the University and himself because, looking forward at this stage, he could not say how much work would be involved for him. The UGC was not keen on such an open-ended situation and admonished UEA to send more regular information. [5]

On the 9th March 1962, in a blaze of publicity - articles or notices in the major national newspapers and in the professional press - Lasdun was formally appointed. Lasdun now claimed to need a year in order to arrive at even a preliminary plan and, according to himself, had 'gone "into purdah"… when…

'A Press Conference was held in Earlham Hall today where plans of the University of East Anglia were released. Mr. Frank Thistlethwaite addressing the conference… seated Mr. Lasdun', 25 April 1963.

planning . Leave us in peace... to seriously consider the nature of these buildings ...' A number of sketches of October 1962 illustrated here and a much more detailed scheme were presented internally in December 1962. The university, on its part, issued a number of what they called 'Cockshy Schedules' which consisted of large amounts of figures, numbers of students, staff, sizes of rooms etc. It appears, however, that these were only of a very preliminary use to Lasdun, at a time when he had hardly done the vaguest planning for the complex overall – while for the UGC they were not detailed enough; all these individual briefs were, in fact, worked out afresh later, from late 1963 onwards. By that time, UEA had opened its 'Village' as a temporary abode which seemed to work extremely well for staff and for the first students – and took attention away from the main project.

According to schedule, Lasdun presented Draft I in April 1963 - again, in an even greater blaze of publicity. The story of Lasdun and UEA now became ever more that of the confident London designer, receiving the widest attention for every detail of his project, on the one hand, and, on the other, the quagmire of the commissioning, designing and building process at Norwich. It was to take another twenty months before building could start. Lasdun had pointed out that 'Draft I' was merely 'an anatomy of ideas', and what was eventually built bore little relationship to it. There is an area of considerable vagueness about Lasdun's brief as such. This was, in fact, typical for the architect-client situation in most of the New Universities: the designers of the Seven prided themselves on assuming an influence in the brief-making process. At UEA and also at Essex this led to statements by the client to the effect that no real brief had ever been given to the architect: Frank Thistlethwaite said, perhaps a little ironically, in a recent interview '... not a college, not a campus, but an Italian hill town, that was Lasdun's brief. Lasdun had no brief'. Thistlethwaite at that point forgot that he supplied, if not an actual brief, very succinct principles of planning to Lasdun, but only for the residences. As to the 'Development Plan' for the whole, such a term is denied by Lasdun, and yet a Proposed Development Plan was issued in Spring 1963, along with Draft I. Briefly stating a number of generalities, it was of little consequence. Ironical-

April 1963; York's first buildings completed for 1965/6. Essex: architect's appointment late 1962, the great plan October 1963, first buildings opened October 1965.

5. Fees: Lasdun said he had not heard of the UGC Fees scale. For him only the RIBA scale was appropriate for individual buildings. He would not accept Town Planning Institute scales for the overall plan because they were designed for men who moved blocks and roads around on a plan. His work for the plan would be much more detailed. Two distinct levels of fees applied: 0.5 % (of the projected 6m ) for the Development Plan, and a slightly reduced fee (from 6 % to 5.75 %) for the buildings; the first set of fees was vital for Lasdun because of the uncertainty as to whether he was to design the buildings. - Sir John Wolfenden, the new UGC Chairman in 1964:

'Mr. Lasdun probably received a rather better financial settlement than any other architect undertaking comparable work' Cf. Peter Yorke (2000): 'In practice Lasdun stuck absolutely to these fees, never claiming additional fees of time spent on this or that as other architects did'.

6. The academic and architectural plan: The Vice Chancellor after his arrival in 1961: 'The First thing to tackle the nature of the curriculum... when that had been decided the architect could be briefed....'; from the following account here one may conclude that this did not happen. Birks is rather misleading in stating 'The result of this brief was a linear plan'. Cf. W. Curtis on Lasdun's National Theatre: 'there was no clear initial brief.' In his own memorandum Lasdun in March 1962 asks: 'Points to discuss with Norwich: Do they accept the challenge to experiment edu

ly, Lasdun provided a Development Plan in 1969, after he had left UEA. Lasdun's 'Drafts' and 'Development Plan' must not be confused; what mattered was the former, that is, the model. Strictly speaking, statements about a 'no plan' or 'no brief' situation cannot make much sense, especially in the case of such a large project. These statements must be taken as an indication that what mattered to the patron, Thistlethwaite, and to the designer, were the high ideals, and not the pedantry of statistics and building details. [6]

It was also particularly difficult at UEA to arrive at a clear definition of the 'client' in these early years. By late 1963 the institution was growing rapidly. There was, of course, always the UGC as the ultimate founder, but this body had no interest in the actual shape of the plan. There were the 'Officers', i.e. The VC and the Registrar; the Estates Bursar (later the Estates Officer); there were the 'governing bodies', Council and Senate, plus the numerous committees of Council or Senate, such as the Buildings Committee or the Site Development Committee. (See the Schedule of Committees below.) As regards the general principles and larger financial issues it was Council which had the final decision, as the body responsible for all non-academic matters. However, it was the Senate which directed all academic matters and thus had the most important influence on the planning of the buildings. There were also the Deans of the Schools, who, as founding deans, had a special say as to the shape of their 'own' buildings. In practice much of the detailed work and technical direction was undertaken by the Estates Officer and his staff. In effect, there was an historical order of appointments to the institution; as we have seen with many of the Seven, it was the team of VC and architect who essentially shaped the campus, especially where the overall architectural scheme was very strong from the start, as at York, Essex and Lancaster. It was also true for UEA, and yet what seemed characteristic at Norwich was the continual strong presence of the local founders of the University who had been there before the officers and who continued to chair Council and its subcommittees. In any case, a great number of the agents were acting as the client, but frequently not in in unison. That was certainly the architect's impression.

cationally and what do they believe the nature of the experiment to be. Do they have views on teaching method and particularly on nature of personal teachers/taught contact. Do they believe that change in a range of knowledge demands different grouping of subjects i.e. do they propose a Schools arrangement as at Sussex or faculties ...?'

The 'Development Plan' contains a mere 2500 words of generalizations about the site, about various uses and the topic of growth, plus the familiar photographs of the models. Thistlethwaite's comment: 'The University's architects have drawn up Development Programmes which makes imaginative provision for the University's long-term requirements'. FT: 'We have a Development Plan'. Lasdun: 'there is no Development Plan.' - Committees: according to Tilsley, the Vice Chancellor was planning, in early 1962, an 'effective pattern of committees'.

7. Murray's internal memo at the UGC on the planner/architect relationship: 'The VC told me that he did not know that the Committee's normal advice was to appoint a consulting architect for general layout and to avoid commitments on individual buildings. I know that at one time I stated this to Lord Mackintosh but I cannot have done so to the VC. Will officers take every opportunity of making this known to universities.'

8. 'Confidential East Anglia:

Mr Cory Dixon [the Estates Officer] called in great distress on the 18th February 1963 to tell Mr Meyrick and me of increasing difficulties which, he said, were arising at East Anglia, and which looked like leading to him, and possibly also his assistant, Mr Marshall looking for other

While there was uncertainty about who was the actual client, no such question applied in the case of the designer, at least not as far as Lasdun was concerned. For most others, however, this, too, was an issue of contention. As already hinted at, way back, in the case of Leslie Martin, there seemed a lack of definition of 'planning': was the architect to be a 'consultant', devising general outlines, to be filled in by subsequent designers? Or was one name to design everything? UEA had been warned that Lasdun was one of the latter kinds of designers. But Mackintosh and Thistlethwaite were on record as having actually stressed 'consistency of design'. During the course of events this was the one quality which even Lasdun's most severe critics were prepared to grant him. The UGC, on the other hand, maintained that one had to begin with a consultant, and that the decisions as to who was to design individual buildings should be taken later. When the UGC learned in early 1962 that Lasdun was likely to want to design everything, Thistlethwaite was admonished by Sir Keith Murray not to proceed 'à la Spence' in Sussex (who was known to have disregarded the UGC financial rules); Thistlethwaite replied that he had not known about the rule. The issue was finally resolved only in October 1963. [7]

In two major phases of squabbles, in Spring 1963 and later on in that year, we can follow in detail the problems faced by all the protagonists. About the first we hear from the reports at the UGC: Cory Dixon, the Estates Bursar came to see them in desperation, complaining that Lasdun did not want to know about him (Dixon) and that the VC and Mackintosh seemed to side with the architect rather than their Estates Bursar. Lasdun had also insisted on seeing the UGC by himself. Dixon specially feared the huge costs. The architects of the UGC remarked afterwards that Dixon was temperamental and prone to exaggeration, but basically they sided with him and decided to try to keep Lasdun under control. They admonished Thistlethwaite to consult the UGC more often and not to push ahead with vague plans. They were even more annoyed when they learned of Lasdun's Draft I through the press, and they now pointed out that the whole architectural undertaking of the University might be in danger. According to Dixon, in an internal UGC memo of 6 of May 1963: 'The Building Committee and the Project Sub-Committee

jobs. In discussion, it appeared that there were three stories of difficulties:-

1stly: Administrative - Mr Cory Dixon had had the greatest possible difficulty in getting information out of the architect, Mr Denys Lasdun, about his plans, and indeed Mr Lasdun virtually refused to admit the existence of the Estate Bursar and his administrative and technical staff. Mr Lasdun, he said, was not prepared to admit any criticism of his plan from Mr Cory Dixon or his staff; he was insisting on having direct access to Heads of Departments without Mr Cory Dixon or a member of his staff being present; he was asking for meetings of the Building Committee from which Mr Cory Dixon would be excluded; and Mr Lasdun was also seeking to get written into his agreement a right of appealing over the heads of the Building Committee to the University Council direct. Furthermore, Mr Lasdun intended that he and his firm should do all the planning of the University, which on present plans represented about £20 million worth of work, and for that purpose to have direct access to the University Grants Committee at any time, without University administrative officers necessarily being present.

2ndly: Financial - Mr Cory Dixon said that Mr Lasdun had made it clear that he intended to tell the University what they should have, and what it would cost. Nothing which Mr Cory Dixon would regard as a development plan had yet been produced, but there were diagrammatic sketches of a large complex of buildings which Mr Cory Dixon estimated might cost as much as £2 million. Mr Cory Dixon had done some calculations based on the usable area which he believed to be required for chemistry, which suggested that an expenditure limit for this area, calculated according to the UGC. formula, would amount only to about 1/3rd of what Mr Lasdun was

had been allowed virtually to lapse and the building programme was now being run by the VC and the architect, with the assistance of two academic members of staff. The VC had stated publicly in a lecture to local architects that he did not intend that the architects should be fettered by committees.' Indeed, the team Lasdun - Thistlethwaite shortly afterwards went to the UGC to talk to Murray in vague and conciliatory terms. Lasdun emphasized that he had so far only produced the first draft of the Development Plan which 'might go through twenty drafts before agreement was finally reached ...'. Murray, however, repeated his warnings that, in effect, UEA might have to start again from scratch. [8]

Five months later Lasdun indeed presented another general scheme of the same kind as Draft I, namely Draft II. This was to bear a greater relationship to the outline of the future building, but still had nothing to do with detailed planning. One large issue appeared to have been solved, namely the position of arts and sciences. Initially the idea was to mix the two. During the summer of 1963, however, the scientists began to demand that all their buildings should be placed together The position of the Arts side was now held to be determined by their position close to the Library. Lasdun in late 1963: 'We were shuffling around all buildings many times... unclear briefing ...'

There now seemed a moment when a greater openness was desirable. The forum was to be Council and the meeting of September 30 1963 marked the high point in Lasdun's client difficulties. The audience was a mixture of academics and 'lay' members. Lasdun delivered his presentation (which was tape-recorded) in the manner of a man confident of his record of service to the University so far, a man who no doubt felt that he was confronting an audience which still needed to be educated as to the complexity and nature of their joint undertaking. 'In my humble view, the university is not geared in the least to what we wanted to do...'. To City Councillor Arthur South, who held forth a great deal and who asked 'Why concrete, why not brick, what colour will your concrete be?' Lasdun replied 'My concrete will be cathedral-coloured.'The fact was that South and some other lay members had been 'ganging up' before the meeting, in order 'to attack, to deflate' the architect. In vain, 'it was a joke... he charmed us all... he

proposing to spend on this part of the complex. It seemed clear that Mr Lasdun intended to "do a Spence" [as at Sussex University] and see that the whole University was created in the way he saw it, regardless of cost.

3rdly: Relations with Local Authorities - Mr Cory Dixon said that Mr Lasdun had entirely refused to discuss his plans with the local Planning Authorities or with the officers of the City Corporation, and that, as a result, a most embarrassing situation was arising. The Local Authorities were asking for information which the Estates Bursar could not give them, and as an example Mr Cory Dixon mentioned that nothing had yet been said to the City Engineer about the points at which access would be needed to the site, or the drainage and sewerage services which would be required. He received constant complaints from the Local Authorities that they were kept wholly in the dark.

Mr Cory Dixon said that the crucial meeting would take place on Wednesday, 20th February, but the present indications were that the Vice-Chancellor and Lord Mackintosh had been wholly won over to Mr Lasdun's view, and intended to support him against their own officers. Mr Meyrick and I comforted Mr Cory Dixon as best we could, while pointing out (as he fully understood) that most of the matters he had mentioned concerned the internal administration of the University, which it was for the University itself to decide. We could, and should, insist that our rules as laid down in the Notes on Procedure were followed and that the buildings were built within the expenditure limit which we should prescribe, but, within that framework, it was for the University to decide how to organize itself. After the meeting Mr Meyrick and I were agreed that there were two sides to the story, and that, as told by the Vice-Chancellor

was so able... not a man one could like... we did not like the buildings he had in mind ...'. Lasdun then restated his planning philosophy: 'My Lord Chairman - before showing you our findings for Draft II - I came into the room at the exact point, I think, when the Vice-Chancellor was talking about the final plan. There is no final plan ever in planning, with respect.' Lasdun acknowledged that there had been considerable unease about the disposition of the science buildings and that questions had been raised by the University and the UGC as to whether or not Lasdun wasn't 'doing too much'. He knew, too, that some people thought he was not operating within UGC procedures; however, there was a letter on file from Sir Keith Murray 'graciously acknowledging that there was no evidence for that anxiety.' On the other hand, Lasdun was quite open, mistakes in planning had been made: 'There would have to have been faults - we are not crystal-gazers.' But then Lasdun went on to air some grievances of his own, such as a lack of consultation over the placing of the Food Research Institute. In Draft 1 (December 1962) the Food Research Institute was on site. In March 1963 the University decided it should be off site. In May 1963 Lasdun was asked to put it back in. And then, without telling Lasdun, the University took it out again. 'Don't you think ultimately that it was an extraordinary piece of behaviour on the part of this University ...'.

The deepest running sore was still the question as to who was to design the first buildings. It was raised by Arthur South and picked up by Lord Mackintosh, who thought that originally it had been agreed that Lasdun would do at least some of the initial buildings - although not to the exclusion of other architects. This enabled Lasdun to jump in and say 'I do not recognize a dichotomy between town planning and architecture. It may be that I am wrong in not having pointed this out in writing, though it was clearly understood - as a gentleman's agreement if you like - that when you approached us at the start I was alerted immediately to what was the role that we were being asked to play, and the point made, but not written, was that we would be entrusted with the first group of buildings.' Thistlethwaite, however, no doubt remembering the way Murray had admonished him in 1962 in this matter, kept stressing that he had not given such an undertaking. [9]

or Mr Lasdun, it would probably sound very different. But even making full allowance for ... exaggeration..., we were left in no doubt that there are likely to be difficulties ahead at East Anglia of the same sort (and possibly even worse) than have arisen at Sussex. For all his faults of temperament, Mr Cory Dixon is one of the most able and experienced Buildings Officer and University Administrators in the country, and what he says cannot be dismissed out of hand. After speaking to Mr Copleston we have given instructions:-(a) that no discussions are to take place with Mr Lasdun or members of his firm without one of our administrators being present; (b) that the rule that correspondence is with the University, and not with firms of architects, is to be rigorously enforced.
20th February, 1963 [Signed] Parnis.'

9. Arthur South: at the meeting September 30 1963 : I really think we must clear the air... There are parts of Mr. Lasdun's talk I cannot understand at all. ...There must be some frank speaking... [councillors] cannot spend the time in coming here discussing things if alongside... are discussions and decisions made on an apparently superior plane'.... 'A Building Committee was formed... ceased to be a responsible committee because its work was done by other people or persons... building committee not informed ...'

During the following months the UGC still warned the university about costliness and the risk that the project might have to be revised ...; communication with Lasdun seemed inadequate; Dixon noted that Lasdun was already preparing detailed designs for some buildings, Dixon and the Registrar noted that the Vice-Chancellor did not seem concerned undu...

The sum of this immensely long and confusing meeting (at one point the Bishop recommended a prayer) was that Lasdun won over the University again to his cause, to his architecture. Thistlethwaite, legalistically, but also diplomatically, reaffirmed the official position that 'the terms of the appointment of the architects made a clear distinction between the work on the Development Plan and the design of the individual buildings, but it had always been understood by the members of the Executive Committee that if things went well, Messrs Lasdun and Partners would be invited to design the core of the first buildings in order to establish the style and character for future developments.' [10]

From this point various members of the Council and its committees did (in principle) take Lasdun's side and deemed that all had gone well, and agreed that the gentleman's agreement should stand and asked Lasdun to try and ensure that the problems of communication, finance and the like were avoided in future. The upshot was another, smaller gathering between Lord Mackintosh, Thistlethwaite, Lasdun and the Registrar. It ended in one simple phrase: 'The University had to trust Lasdun'. From now one gets a better idea of different client groups within the institution. Cory Dixon handed in his notice in November 1963 and subsequently took up a post at the University of Surrey and later wrote a book about commissioning buildings for universities. The Vice Chancellor re-established himself again as the chief client, a patron, 'almost in an eighteenth century way'. He and his architect represented 'a meeting of minds'. At the same time more individual user groups began to formulate their needs. From now all appeared plain sailing. In November 1963 Lasdun received an accolade from the Site Development Committee: 'Your plan accurately reflects academic brief, [it is] indeed a brilliant formulation in architectural terms of the University's grand academic design'. All the major parties produced detailed schedules. It was now up to the academic staff to make sure they obtained the spaces they needed. Much praised by both the University and by Lasdun was Willi Guttsman, the founder Librarian: He 'was a wizard in thinking how to get the best library from a limited budget. He was very firm with Lasdun. Willi as the client did a heroic job. He was good at devising economies that did not affect the quality of the architec-

and seemed to think the problems can be solved by a discussion between Murray, the architect and himself (FT).

Peter Yorke comments (1997): 'Dixon was hardly exaggerating... Most architects do a lot of apparently very detailed design (in order to get their minds clear on what they want or whether t is feasible) before they have been commissioned. The fear is that they'll then want paying even f it turns out to have been abortive. This risk seems inherent in a process of producing innovatory designs.'

10. Lasdun's 'conditions': 1) If the University decided not to offer his firm all the buildings in the rst group he and his partners would have to consider whether they would do any of the build-

ings; it was essential that the first buildings should have a coherent style and form a fitting nucleus for the future. 2) If Lasdun's firm was allowed to do the first group of buildings it would mean they would be employed by the University for seven years, after which the University would probably 'have had enough of Lasdun'. 3) He would not trust other architects at this stage although once the form and style of the buildings had been established it would be possible to bring them in later. 4) Lasdun was working on a novel principle of industrial construction for the teaching buildings. Once established, other architects could use this system. 5) The University had to trust Lasdun. If these conditions were accepted then he would continue as the University's architect.

The UGC in late 1964: 'The whole history of planning at UEA is deplorable. We were not

ture...' (James Macfarlane). It was January 1965 when building could finally begin on University Plain. [11]

However, it was now, one might say, that the real problems began. Of the buildings that were to be opened by October 1966: Biology, Arts Block I, Library, University House, Boiler House, Chemistry and the first few blocks of the Residences, only the last three were completed, and that barely. Biology and Arts I had to wait to October 1967, and the Library and Computing Centre came on stream only a year after that. The problem now was essentially that the University wanted more money than the UGC could afford. In Spring 1967, the VC asked for £4 m. for the current programme. Lasdun's buildings, he argued, had to be built together. But the UGC could give only somewhat more than half of it, amounting to about £1 m per year and thus building the Library and University House had to be postponed. The latter's planning process represented, moreover, a record of client indecision. Furthermore, from 1966 the UGC exercised stricter control of building projects. The government asked all universities to cram more students into existing buildings. And from the beginning of 1968 the UGC was entitled to see each university's books. Lasdun put in designs for low-price residences and he claimed that his Lecture Theatre block had been built exceptionally cheaply. It became certain that some existing modes of building could not be afforded any more. The most serious hiatus emerged in 1968 when it turned out that, because of expense, the linking part of the Teaching Wall, the Mathematics and Physics Building, could not be built as Lasdun was planning it, a major blow, of course, to the concept of unity. By mid-1968, a general government moratorium was issued and nobody knew the building allowances for the following year; UEA's and Lasdun's bad luck was that the period of their most intensive building fell into a period when the high wave of new university enthusiasm was practically over. [12]

It was a combination of UEA's tardiness and the bleakness of government finance that brought the architect - client difficulties to a head once again during late 1968. At the same time the University authorities became concerned about their own procedures, too; it was felt, by Gordon Marshall, the Estates

consulted about their plan until the University were publicly committed to it; ...Mr Cory Dixon... was trying to keep matters under proper financial control; they have proceeded in disregard of every warning given to them and now, not surprisingly, they are in the jam which others have foreseen and avoided'.

11. Peter Yorke (1997/2000): 'From 1963/4 briefing lists became more detailed... with the twin tasks of making the new Schools work in the Village, and making sense of the hazy outlines of the buildings being planned on the Plain. Of the three main teaching buildings, CHE pressed ahead ruthlessly, reflecting the dominance of Alan Katritzky whose School was a year younger than BIO but got its building finished a year earlier, in October 1966. BIO was the subject of many

changes of plan, as the departmental structure within the School struggled to make practica reality of the idea of one main upper floor for each major division of the subject. The plan for Arts I went through enormous numbers of revisions as the original 1963 ideas of schools and their numbers of staff and students changed during 1964-6; the problem being again that the Schools constantly revised their sizes, so the floor layout plans went through multiple revisions Throughout these early years, the building plans were supervised by Building Committees with quite large membership from the "users", who therefore acquired a constitutionally legiti mated say in the detailed design of the building. This was a mistake, in leading to too much purpose-design, and a vulnerability to individual mind-changing, and it was rectified by new rules made by Roy Campbell as Pro-VC, which are still in force, whereby only one representative c

Officer, that the old ways of planning and briefmaking were no longer adequate. The fact was that UEA, alone among the New Universities had not yet committed the £ 6.5 m. originally envisaged, but only £4 m. And there was, of course, the general malaise which had befallen the New Universities and their architecture. Lasdun himself, however, was on the crest of a wave; his reputation had risen considerably since he had taken on UEA and it would seem that he himself had lost interest in fighting with those increasingly stricter government norms. He had never accepted that discipline, he always believed he had to try and circumvent it; the 'poetry of architecture' was more important to him than UGC yardsticks. Finally, for the users of the University the situation was confused, and partly defused, by the way in which, even by 1970, most activities were still happily conducted in the Village. [13]

By late 1968 the University had formed a special Committee on the Relationship with the Architect. It met in great secrecy, and for legal reasons it is still not possible to reveal its precise contents. Furthermore, a number of documents relating to this period were not made available to the authors. Further research needs to establish exactly what worried UEA's authorities, beyond the kinds of problems that are common on most large building sites. Certainly, as we noted above, Lasdun had his complaints about the client, too. However, there was, as in all important phases of the UEA-architect relationship, a smooth public face to the internal quagmire. The Newsletter of 22 November 1968 stated: 'From the outset, Mr Lasdun proposed to Council that once the principles of the Development Plan had been accepted and the basic design and form of the University established, other architects should continue with the work. Following discussions with Mr Lasdun, Council has agreed with him that this would be an appropriate time to implement these intentions.' These words are so low key, one has to read them twice to grasp the fact that Lasdun was leaving. It was agreed, on Lasdun's insistence, that no publicity and no explanation should be given to the press or the public. Lasdun's stipulation of no publicity was absolute. 'If the Council guns fired in the wrong direction, he would act.' What, someone asked Lasdun, if the architectural correspondent of the *Daily Telegraph* telephoned for information? Las-

The Site (the Municipal Golf Course), view towards the River Yare. In the early years the campus was called 'University Plain', with reference to an ancient Norwich use of the word for an urban open space, as in Dutch 'plein'.

the future users has to agree the detailed brief with architects via the Estates Division. Thus instructions are now controlled by being fed via a restricted and professional channel. This was not the case in 1964-6. One wonders how much the inexperience of all at UEA in those years, Thistlethwaite included, led to the troubled relationship of the later Lasdun years.'

An example of indecision: 'University House' on University Plain. 'Sketch Design, March 1967' lists approximately 18 changes, major or minor, in the planning process between August 1962 and January 1967. - This is from the assessment by the architect. FT admitted as much in principle in his (public) VC's Report: '... delay in having a social centre due in part to the difficulty of designing so complex a project and in part to successive deferments of building allocations'. Finally, the moratorium of 1968 delayed it again.

Peter Yorke (1997): 'One has to also bear in mind the very real difficulty in forecasting in 1963/4 the ways in which university administration would develop by 1966/7... the demands for space from such institutions as Deans of Students... However, the proximate cause of the abandonment of the project, which I minuted, was that the cost exceeded the UGC cost limit by too great a margin ...., i.e. it was back to the architect.'

12. Lasdun (in 1996) confirmed that 'he did not make it his job' to do what the UGC wanted, i.e. to stay within the financial guidelines. Lasdun tried to operate frequently, though of course not illegitimately, with 'Abnormals', i.e. one could go to the UGC with requests for extras (such as site difficulties), which were not contained in the UGC's Guidelines and cost ceilings for the

dun replied that the man should be referred to him immediately. 'If anybody gave a public answer out of line with the spirit of this meeting, then there would be a reaction from him.'

It is not, of course, the purpose of this chapter to discuss who was right in this dispute - if indeed one can speak of a real, major dispute at all. There were several factors responsible for the lack of speed in Norwich. Lasdun usually took longer than many other architects with his design process. He can claim that his design philosophy of complexity within unity does take a greater design effort. At Kent, for instance, the problem of creating a design unity between some of the out-of-sight science buildings and the colleges simply did not arise. Overall planning and design unity was never even intended. On the other hand, the material factors of the multifariousness of the UEA client and the small size of Lasdun's office also played a major part in the delays. Lastly, the Lasdun-UEA disputes still formed part of the national/local dichotomy which constitutes one of the sub-themes of this book. 1968 saw a re-emergence of the polarization which had already dominated the year 1963: a metropolitan architect as well as a carefully staged face towards the outside, to the national press, the metropolitan circle of colleagues - in this case a carefully staged non-publicity, versus local patrons and local concerns. The Committee on the Relationship with the Architect was a Committee of Council and it was ruled by the likes of Sir Edmund Bacon (its Chairman) or Timothy Colman who feared for a misuse of the remainder of the local appeal money he had helped to collect in 1962-3. These 'lay members' had helped to appoint the modern architect Lasdun in 1961-2; now they were perhaps slightly disillusioned by the wave of low esteem afforded to that style of architecture. The story of UEA architecture continues with the designer of their choice, the local architect Feilden, which turned out to be a very satisfactory choice in their own and in the university users' terms. However, the decision did not gain the Norwich elite great standing as national patrons of architecture.

How does one sum up such a complex story? For the client's part this seems simple enough: UEA acted in an autocratic as well as in a democratic way. Lasdun, on his part, strove for utmost consistency

---

kind of building in question; Lasdun also tried to squeeze out more from the 'equipment grant. J.MacFarlane (1997): 'Lasdun never understood the power of the UGC norms. He felt that if you could argue with the UGC and win your case on part of the project then this was good. Lasdun was after victories on individual buildings, but the UGC always clawed back on subsequent buildings'.

Peter Yorke (1997): 'Generally the UGC maintained that the UEA had a building programme allocation of £6 m. The finally agreed cost of each project was debited to this £6m. Arts 1 had an abnormal addition to its expenditure limit for the "structure only bay". This was a dodge - quite sensible in practice - to get extra money for building the last bit of the Arts Teaching Wing, but not to fit it out (hence "structure only"). It was fitted out as the part of the Arts II project, but that project had an amount corresponding to the Arts I addition deducted from its expenditure limit. Reverting to the "Building Programme", an immense amount of effort went into accounting for it, reconciling it with UGC figures, and reporting on it to committees - since it was all, in effect, UEA capital and had to be closely watched'. Who would have foreseen that the relationship architect - client - UGC was to lead to such gymnastics?'

*The Times* 1 April 1968: the reduced UGC allocation for UEA now fixed at £7 m up to 1972, more than £2 m less than asked for. In 1969 Feilden claimed generally that every day of delay had wasted £500.

13. From report of Lasdun's reply to the University [summarised]: What existed on the University Plain had got a body of opinion which recognized its merits and was of value to the

in design, but at the same time kept changing the details. One might argue that architect and client, i.e. UEA as a client group, rarely 'met'; few at UEA had a real understanding of the style of Lasdun's design; while Lasdun was not really interested in his clients as a specific group of people, although he had a strong notion of the generic user of his buildings, something to be explored in the next section. The final question that arises at Lasdun's UEA is surely this: How could buildings which attracted such strong architectural acclaim originate from such a contorted story? It was because of those amongst the client group who never wavered in their belief in the importance of the architecture 'as such', above all the Vice Chancellor, but also all those in Lasdun's office and in the technical and administrative offices at UEA whose professional competence in dealing with the day to day processes of building (regardless of the architectural style) had made sure the grand design stood up and was paid for. [13]

Lasdun's University of East Anglia is clearly one of those cases of architectural patronage and design where one has to step back a long way to find a positive evaluation, step back, that is, from the reality of the building process and the experience of the state of incompleteness when it was first used. It was probably highly significant that nobody, neither the University authorities, nor the architect, nor the first users, felt inclined at the time to mark the 'opening' of the great campus - as UEA had done at the 'Village' and as was to happen with the Sainsbury Centre. Lasdun received by far his greatest praise at the stage of the great models. 'Draft I' in 1963 marked the high point of enthusiasm in the architectural world: 'The Universal University. A Leap into the Future' was the introductory title of the *Architectural Review's* special number on the New Universities in October of that year, featuring the UEA residences, as well as Lasdun's expansion models (cf. page 10) on its cover. In the same month the grandiose plan of Essex burst on the scene. About UEA Lionel Brett, one of the *Review's* most distinguished critics wrote: 'Lasdun's very first step was intuitive... a deeply felt and imaginative concept... compactness is intensified... The veins of this beautiful organism are to fill with blood, pumped systematically from the heart... [will] give variety and vitality to the fabric of a great cathedral.' A year later Michael Cassidy, a teacher of

university as well as to its architects. However, he did not want to discuss laurels. His concern was with the future. Were Denys Lasdun and Partners being asked to do something very different? Were they being asked to step aside as Development Plan Architects, letting expediency and squalor follow their departure? To whom would he be handing over and what steps could the Council take to avoid a 'creeping devaluation of the environment?' Most important of all, Lasdun explained that he could not design downwards just to meet the cost constraints of the present; he had a duty to design for future buildings of which the University could be proud.

In 1985 Frank Thistlethwaite was given an Honorary Membership of the Royal Institute British Architects.

**F.Thistlethwaite DENYS LASDUN AND THE DEVELOPMENT PLAN(1996):**
"I had always taken a serious interest in architecture and indeed as a schoolboy wished to become an architect. The opportunity to have a principal hand in building a whole university was therefore one which I especially relished. Throughout my many years in Cambridge I never lost the sense of being surrounded by good or at least interesting buildings, courts and grounds; and my ambition for UEA was to provide us, both faculty and students, with an architectonic presence.

For our bombed-out War generation, the modern movement, from the Bauhaus onwards, was exciting and its buildings promised a creative future. That green field golf course at Earlham provided a rare opportunity to build a modern idiom suitable for a new University. I wanted the best contemporary architecture of its time: distinguished buildings which would make a pos-

architecture at the Bartlett School of Architecture in London stressed more the sociological aspects: 'UEA have rethought the socio-academic relationship... The intellectual consistency and architectural rigour of the planning for Norwich and Colchester represent the first examples of real solutions to the new conditions facing higher education'. During the following years admiration of the 'outside world', that is, of top architectural journals did not diminish: Joseph Rykwert, an architectural theoretitian, soon to teach at Essex, wrote in the Italian yearbook *Zodiac* about the newest style of planning, the 'linear character' which East Anglia 'comes nearest to'. Generally, the new wave of university buildings represented to Rykwert the 'archetype or paradigm' of those years, like 'the Cathedrals of the Middle Ages'. He concludes with a plea for the architect's 'freedom', which he likens generally to the 'free expression of disagreement as a token of that humanity'. Soon, however, the image of all the New Universties became tainted. The criticism of Tony Birks and others will be discussed in a further section; but for him, too, UEA was the 'most romantic and intellectually appealing of the Seven'. 'Heroic' was the term proposed at the beginning of this book to characterise the efforts of the 1960s; it can be taken to mean something admirable and astonishing, but also as referring to an unfortunate gap between vision and reality.

itive presence felt and provide a sense of place and an aesthetic experience for generations of students. I also wanted the University to have a unity of design: I was not enamoured of the miscellany of buildings and styles on the average Redbrick campus. I was therefore anxious to have an architect capable of designing, or at least setting his seal on, the whole university development plan.

One of the functions of the Academic Planning Board was to recommend to the University's promoters the appointment of an architect. Before I joined them our Planning Board had already invited Sir Leslie Martin, the Professor of Architecture in Cambridge, and he had declined. Instead Charles Wilson, our chairman, recommended Denys Lasdun who had been his client for a hall of residence at Leicester. This was early in Lasdun's career before he had become widely known for major buildings although I think at the time he was already at work on his brilliant Royal College of Physicians in Regent's Park. He was also known to me as the runner-up in a limited competition for the design of the new Cripps Court of student rooms in St. John's College. I had been a member of the building committee for this and had been particularly attracted by the originality of the Lasdun stepped-back design. I realized that although something as uncompromisingly 'Modern' as this might not be suitable for the Cambridge Backs, just such a building would be appropriate at Earlham and its architect might well be the man we were looking for. I think other members of the Board also had experience of Lasdun's work: And so, without much further ado I was sent off to talk to him. We met on 10th October 1961 at his small office then in Albany Street. We liked each other and he was attracted by what would of course be a major commission. The Planning Board duly recommended him to the Promotion Committee who appointed him Consultant Architect for the Development Plan of the University.

At the start Lasdun told us he would need a year before bringing design proposals to us. He was right; and it was fortunate that our decision to build a 'village' as I mis-called it, of temporary huts (greatly against the advice of my older vice-chancellor colleagues) enabled us both to accept students quickly and give the architect a proper amount of design time. The brief I gave him, which I had set out on a page or so for the Planning Board, was indeed brief. Having taken the strategic decision not to be a collegiate university, I stipulated that it should be as unified a community as possible; students would identify socially on the one hand with their School of Study and on the other not with a college or 'hall of residence' but with their staircase with a notional unit of twelve students on each floor. My concept (Thistlethwaite agreed with Lasdun in August 2000 that this should be altered to 'The architect's concept') was urban: buildings linked with walkways, square and street, free from traffic, rather like an Italian Renaissance town. This would also have the advantage of concentrating the university and freeing the maximum acreage of the Earlham site as decorative parkland with a hint of Humphrey Repton. That was about as much of a briefing as I ever gave Denys; but he seemed to think it sufficient and indeed has said he appreciated me as client. He certainly designed brilliantly within it. The original St. John's building which had so taken my fancy re-emerged as the ziggurats of Norfolk and Suffolk Terraces. The abbreviation 'UEA' derives from the cartouches of Lasdun and Partners' working drawings. It gave me great satisfaction when Sir Denys Lasdun was awarded the RIBA Gold Medal, the first of three of our architects to be so distinguished.

I have to record that there was another idea in the air at the time which emerged from school architecture: that buildings should be functional units, systematically manufactured for purposes which would alter and therefore should have only a limited life. The University of York went down this road, system building called CLASP, which was much approved of by the Treasury because, of course, it was cheap. I would have none of it. However, the concept of a building with a life limited to thirty years was, alas, Treasury policy and a scandal from which the country has not recovered." (from: F.T., *Origins*...publ. F.T., Cambridge 2000)

## UEA: A SURVEY OF SOME COMMITTEES IN THE 1960s

with special emphasis on building committees:

[Local] University Promotion
Committee 1959
Executive Sub-Committtee

### EXECUTIVE COMMITTEE 1960

Buildings (Sub) Committee 5-12-
1962
Ad hoc Comm. on the Appointment
of the Architect
Project Sub Committees

### ACADEMIC PLANNING
BOARD (UGC appointed)

### COMMITTEES OF COUNCIL
(largely 'lay') from 23-4-1964

Site Development Committee of
Council 1964-7 with Sub-Comm. on
Arts, Chemistry, Library, Residences,
University House, Fabric
Site Sub-Comm. 1964
Finance and General Purposes
Committee 1965
Ad hoc Comm. on the Relationship
with the Architect 1968
Planning Committee of Council 1969

### COMMITTEES OF SENATE
(academic) from 11-3-1963

(Site) Development Comm. of
Senate 1-4-1963
Development Committee

Planning Sub-Comm. 1966

### LASDUN: BUILDING PROGRAMME UEA:

October 1962: preliminary sketches; April 1963: 'Development Plan Drafts
', Models, short booklet; Autumn 1963: 'Development Plan Draft II' Model; October 1963: 'provisional Building Programme'; Detailed Programmes
and Estimates from 1964; D.Lasdun [Retrospective] Development Plan
June 1969; B.Feilden, Development Plan II, April 1970.

### MAIN CONTRACTORS:

Site Works: W.H.Monk; Residences: Gazes of Kingston; Chemistry,
Biology, Arts I, II: R.G.Carter of Drayton (Norwich); Library I, Lecture
Theatres: Costain Construction. Carter remained by far the most important contractor at UEA. For a complete list of Lasdun's contractors,
builders, manufacturers: *Architectural Review* April 1970, pp. 312-3.

### SENIOR UEA STAFF CONCERNED WITH BUILDINGS:

1964/5: Estates Officer, 2 Assistant Estates Officers, Senior Clerk of
Works (Total 4)
1967: Estates Officer, Deputy Estates Officer, Maintenance Officer and
Engineer, Assistant Estates officer, Administrative Assistants (3), Safe-
ty Officer, Senior Clerk of Works (total 9).

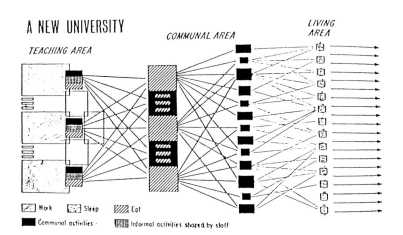

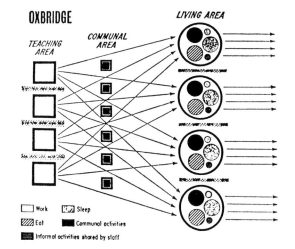

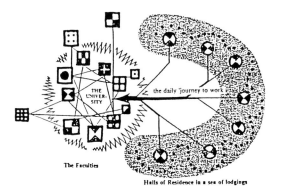

SOCIOGRAMS OF UNIVERSITY
LIFE, 1960s
The period abounds in this kind
of diagrammatic drawing which
is meant, above all, to underline
the togetherness of all at the
university. The diagrams above
and left of 1964, are by the
sociologist Peter Marris, and
aim to demonstrate the greater
togetherness in a new
university plan, while the
drawing below, from the
Development Plan of the
University of York of 1962,
caricatures the dispersal of life
in virtually all universities
outside Oxbridge.

## THE ARCHITECTURE OF THE SEVEN

Although it is hard to guage this from their schematised plans, the most astonishing feature of the Seven is their diversity. They are strongly divergent in their institutional formation and utterly different in their architectural planning. It is not easy to establish a chronological sequence of planning style.

Arguably, the last major plan, that of Warwick, by Yorke, Rosenberg & Mardall (YRM) of late 1964 is the most old-fashioned in the way it adopts a mode of Modernism prevalent from the 1930s into the 1950s and early 1960s, that of the rectangular block formation, a type that was adopted by the great majority of new universities all over the world. The rectangular slab is indeed one of the most economic types of building. The second most important issue is the rational accomodation of vehicular traffic, by simply adopting an ample network of straight roads. Warwick, in effect, in its original parts, resembles a 'Modern' office town.

The very opposite, in some ways, was Sussex, designed by Basil Spence five years before Warwick, in 1959. Sussex was held to be the first major English campus layout, campus meaning here an irregular, and on the whole gentle, sprinkling of buildings in an existing park. The quad-like plans of some buildings, however, are strongly reminiscent of Oxbridge.

A rather different kind of plan was provided by those who opted for the college model. Kent, designed by Sir William Holford from 1963, saw the University as a series of self-contained colleges, with a number of teaching and adminstrative buildings occupying the rest of the site.

It was York, designed in early 1962 by Robert Matthew, Johnson-Marshall (with Andrew Derbyshire in charge) which most systematically took on the college model, but also modified it in order to link the individual colleges together within a landscaped park, as at Sussex. Thus, in contrast to Kent's fortresses, the York colleges show a rather open and spread-out character.

The really radical group among the seven is constituted by East Anglia, Essex (Architects' Co-Partnership with Kenneth Capon in charge) and Lancaster (Bridgwater, Shepheard and Epstein, with Gabriel Epstein in charge), all essentially designed in early to mid-1963, though East Anglia was publicised some way ahead of the other two. The three reject virtually all earlier modes of university design, the campus, in the sense of a large area sprinkled with diverse buildings (the normal American and Sussex's procedure); the old English Civic or Redbrick types of massive centralised buildings; the pure Oxbridge type of college, as well as the 'Modernist' rectangular block type of the Warwick plan. Norwich, Essex and Lancaster adhere to a new concept: a university should essentially be one vast building. Only in this way could the unity of the institution and its aims, academic and educational co-operation, be achieved. That said, the plans of the three look completely different from each other. The chief difference between East Anglia and the other two is the way Lasdun strung out his components, as a series of lines closely placed together, whereas Essex and Lancaster appear more like a dense net or mesh. Lancaster, moreover, did adopt, like York and Kent, some major elements of the college mode, but then linked them in the whole much more strongly than the other two. An important common feature of the three is the strict separation of vehicular and pedestrian traffic. But what East Anglia, Essex and Lancaster share most of all is not contained so much in their actual architectural form, but in the way the users are meant to move around in them; these campuses are, in fact, understood as compact, self-contained, small towns.

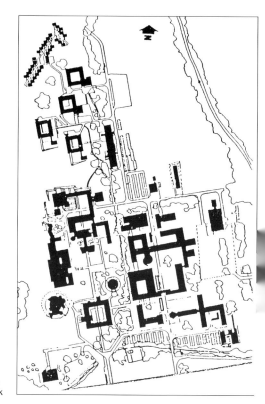

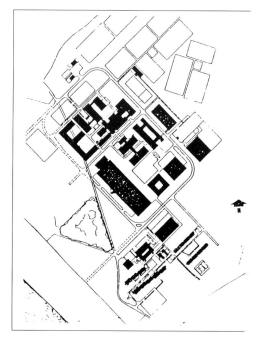

Above: Sussex
Below: Warwick

64

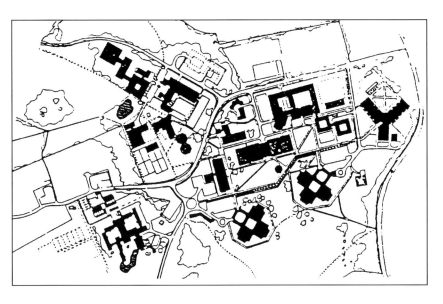
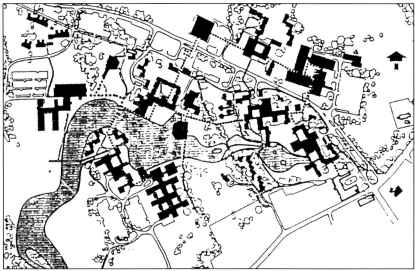

Above: (left) **Kent**, (right) **York**.
Below: **Essex**, **UEA**, **Lancaster**.

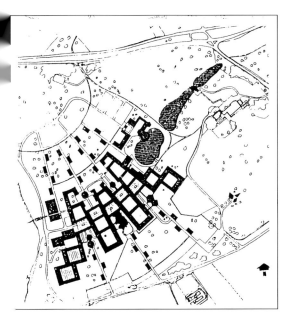
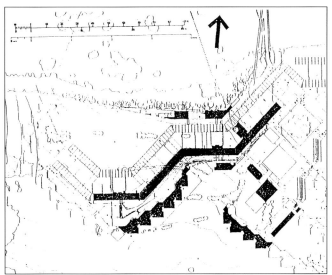
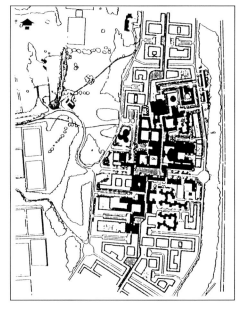

## DENYS LASDUN: PRECURSORS TO THE UEA PLAN

Analyses of Lasdun's mature work begin with Hallfield School as it shows for the first time an 'antidiagrammatic' layout, i.e. it breaks with Classic Modernist rectiliniarity. (The sense of 'diagrammatic' thus varies from the way the term was used above.) The wings of the school form a 'harbour' which is meant to give the users a certain kind of spatial, and thus psychological comfort. It takes part in a trend of Modern architecture which has been called 'organic', in contrast to other kinds of Modernist design characterised as mechanical. In the plan for Fitzwilliam College Lasdun combines the traditional form of the quad with the 'organic' form of a spiral in order to increase the visual togetherness of the various college functions. The large block in the centre is the Dining Hall. (Cf. also his other early designs for Cambridge below, page 85).

Left from top: Drawing of Plants, c.1950s
Hallfield School, plan (Bishops Bridge Road Paddington, London) from 1951.
Fitzwilliam College Cambridge, plan of 1959.
Right: Three early Sketches for UEA, October 1962.

Opposite: 'Development Plan', 'Draft I' April 1993. 'An anatomy of ideas'... 'arts and sciences intermingled'.

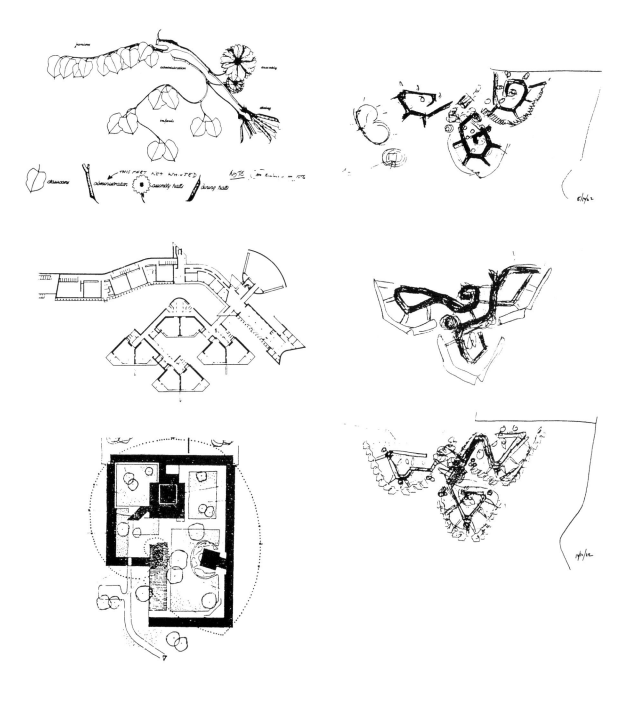

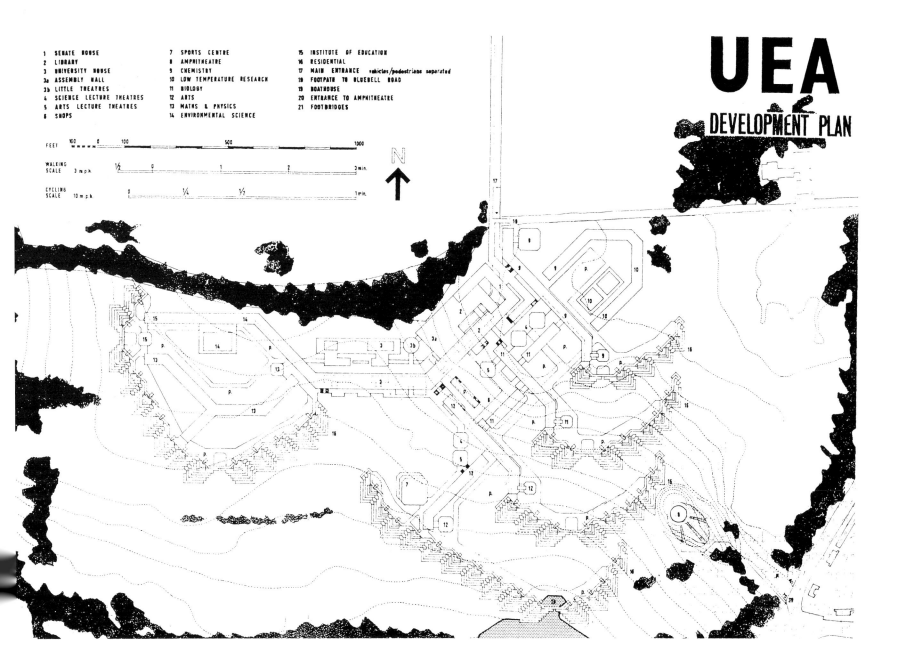

1 SENATE HOUSE
2 LIBRARY
3 UNIVERSITY HOUSE
3a ASSEMBLY HALL
3b LITTLE THEATRES
4 SCIENCE LECTURE THEATRES
5 ARTS LECTURE THEATRES
6 SHOPS
7 SPORTS CENTRE
8 AMPHITHEATRE
9 CHEMISTRY
10 LOW TEMPERATURE RESEARCH
11 BIOLOGY
12 ARTS
13 MATHS & PHYSICS
14 ENVIRONMENTAL SCIENCE
15 INSTITUTE OF EDUCATION
16 RESIDENTIAL
17 MAIN ENTRANCE vehicles/pedestrians separated
18 FOOTPATH TO BLUEBELL ROAD
19 BOATHOUSE
20 ENTRANCE TO AMPHITHEATRE
21 FOOTBRIDGES

FEET  100  0  100  500  1000

WALKING SCALE  3 m.p.h.   ½  0  1  2  2 min.

CYCLING SCALE  10 m.p.h.   0  ¼  ½  1 min.

N

# UEA
## DEVELOPMENT PLAN

Opposite: 'Draft I', Model, one of the celebrated photos, April 1963.

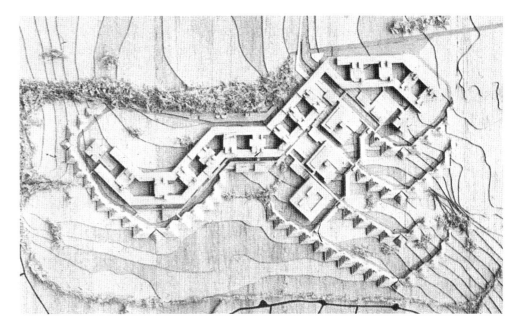

Above: 'Draft II', late 1963.
Below: Preliminary Model corresponding to the centre of Draft I (UEA Building Archives); it was hardly publicised.

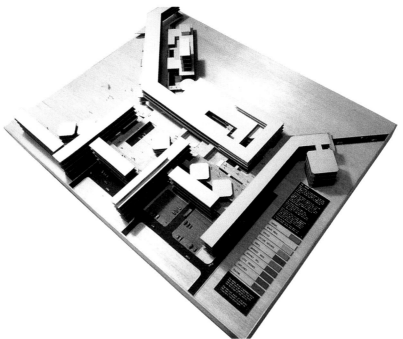

## CONSTRUCTION IN REINFORCED CONCRETE

Among the architects of his generation, Lasdun does not belong to those who go for a particularly daring use of Modern materials. Like many Post-WWII designers, following the lead of Le Corbusier's later work, Lasdun prefers concrete and he prefers his concrete to look solid rather than delicate. Lasdun's buildings never aspire to great height, but he does not like them to sit squarely on the ground either. Load-bearing walls hardly belong to his design vocabulary. He prefers horizontal bands between windows, projecting slabs and vast platforms ('strata'), cantilevered or on stilts, as well as long pedestrian bridges. Reinforced concrete provides the natural construction for almost all these forms.

It is one of the principal beliefs of Modernist architecture that the design concept and its material realisation should be integrated as closely as possible. The essential construction of a building and its surface appearance should be one. (A glance at Mather's nearby Post-Modernist Education School and its cladded walls provides a useful contrast.) Like Lasdun's National Theatre, his University has become a monument to its material.

Lasdun usually objects when he is counted in with Brutalism, or the English 'New Brutalist' movement of the late 1950s, although the 'constructional ethic' just outlined was one of Brutalism's important credos. Lasdun also does, or did, as the Brutalists, believe in a basic value of concrete, namely that it requires no maintenance. Furthermore, in a Corbusierian sense he manipulates texture and colour. At UEA, however, he speaks (in 1969) of a 'natural colour' ('80-20 grey and white cement and Leamoor sand'). 'The infinite variety of colour in the valley landscape makes the choice of external materials and colour of particular importance. Of all the suitable materials available today concrete in its natural grey state appears to enhance the colours of the landscape to greatest advantage.'

A particular issue in reinforced concrete construction was the prefabrication and 'dry' assembly of large components. Here Lasdun took part in a wave of efforts that swept Britain in the early 1960s which not only aimed at the cheapest and most efficient building method, but also believed in the 'modular', as well as in the industrialised nature of all building. In true Modernist thinking, such a systematic approach helped with a unified appearance of all buildings. In particular, the 'cellular' structure of housing seemed to suggest the construction of the whole fabric out of prefabricated panels. In the case of the Residences' external cladding they were manufactured on site (in Lytag Concrete); in the case of the Teaching Block the panels were produced in a factory. The concrete or metal used in the actual formwork, that is in the actual moulds, accounts for a smoother surface finish than in those parts of the buildings, for instance the 'towers', which were cast in situ, using wooden formwork. Inside, the concrete panels were initially plastered and painted; increasingly, though, they were covered only with emulsion, or left as they are, thus preserving the unified look of the construction throughout (as well as saving money). The Teaching Blocks and the Library contain a greater proportion of in situ concrete. Structural Engineers: Ove Arup & Partners; contractors for the Teaching Wall R.G.Carter.

UEA was altogether one of the largest projects of this kind of prefabrication. But it was Lasdun himself who designed his system to suit the particular forms he wanted. By choosing an 'ad-hoc closed structural system', Lasdun sided with the architects' faction in the pursuit of prefabrication, while the UGC had argued for buying in a system which would have suggested greater economies of scale, e.g. CLASP, as adopted by York. With Norfolk being a centre of concrete prefabrication (at Lenwade), Lasdun could actually point to the local benefits of his concept. (Anglian Building Products supplied parts for the Library and the Teaching Block). Whether, in the end, it was more economical than using conventional kinds of construction for the same amount of accommodation would be hard to assess. Certainly CLASP did not turn out to be cheap; on the other hand, most New University construction did keep within UGC/Government cost limits, of the early 1960s, that is. Soon Lancaster decided for conventional construction in its low to medium-rise building and Feilden's UEA structures of the 1970s are built mostly in cheap concrete blockwork.

Concrete, however, is also held to cause problems. Some are constructional, such as 'spalling', i.e. the way the outer surface can fall off, which exposes the metal reinforcement to the elements, with the result of rust attacking the metalwork inside. A more pervasive problem - which is hard to remedy by maintenance - is the disfiguration of the surfaces by rainwater. Lasdun is on record as actually liking these occurrences: when discussing his National Theatre, he maintained that concrete '... will weather,... will streak, it will become part of nature.' But it hardly needs emphasising that streaking from the rain and other kinds of blotches on concrete surfaces were among the least popular visual elements of Modernist architecture - with the general public as well as with the profession. There is a crucial difference between in situ poured concrete and pre-cast concrete. With the latter there is a greater opportunity to manipulate surface and colour. Moreover, Lasdun had himself devised a method whereby for his outer prefabricated panels, rainwater is drained away from the surface by inbuilt methods, so as to minimise streaking. Lasdun used it for his St James's Place Flats, London 1960; at UEA this would have been too expensive. The mix and the smoother surfacing of the pre-cast panels are in any case more streak-resistant than the sheer surfaces of in situ concrete. The remedies that were proposed from the late 1960s for both kinds of concrete were to manipulate the colours of the concrete and to give all surfaces a relief structure. Lasdun's towers at UEA, in a way, carry on an earlier Modernist style where pure form and smooth surfaces predominated. But in Classic Interwar Modernism those surfaces were always meant to be ultra smooth and painted an absolutely clean white, not dark and blotchy. Subsequent to UEA Lasdun practised two different modes. The smooth and lightly coloured pre-cast panels of Christ's College, Cambridge are free of weather problems, whereas at the National Theatre Classical Modernism's uncompromising roughly surfaced cubes celebrated their last manifestation.

Construction Diagrams of Teaching Block and
Residences, 1965-6.
Below: Residences under Construction 1965/6.

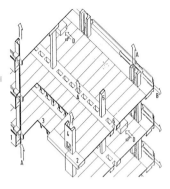

Teaching and Research
Accommodation
Structure and Services

1 Precast concrete spandrel panel
2 Precast concrete edge beam
3 Precast concrete tee beam
4 Precast concrete column
5 In situ concrete column
6 In situ spine beam allowing
   penetration by services

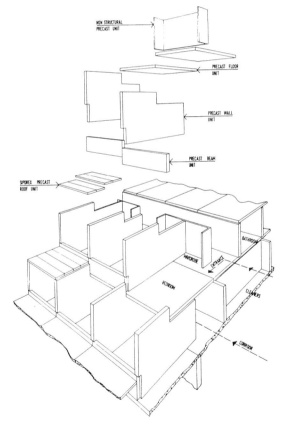

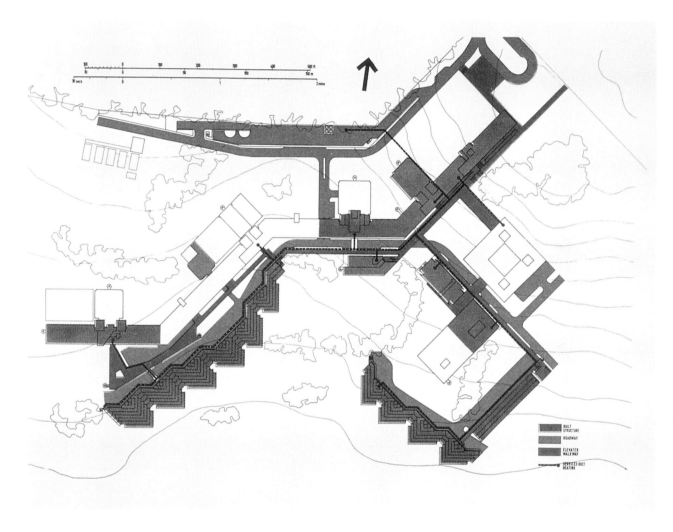

BUILT
STRUCTURE
ROADWAY
ELEVATED
WALKWAY
SERVICES DUCT
HEATING

## PLANNING THE CAMPUS AS A COMPLETE ENTITY.

To use just the term 'plan' would be choosing too mean a word to cover the totality of the architect's efforts. Lasdun was quoted above to the effect that there was no such thing as a complete plan; creating a large building complex does not proceed by devising a quasi-two-dimensional layout and then just building upwards. The activities of planning and design constitute a seamless whole.

To comprehend Lasdun's UEA one cannot do better than to take an aerial view. This is, of course, the way models are meant to work. Draft II came closer to the eventual layout, but it is important to note that in the course of the detailed planning and the building of the various parts Lasdun changed his conception of the whole. Partly this was due to the fact that the size of the whole, and the number of its parts, had to be reduced considerably - as with all the New Universities. But for UEA this also meant a greatly reduced overall density, a reduction of the massed grouping of Draft I; instead, the complex now appears much more elongated. Lasdun increasingly argued for the penetration of the landscape into the building complex; he spoke of 'swathes' and 'landlocked harbours'. At the same time this demanded even more care about the 'linkages', i.e. the walkway system, a network in its own right as well as the crucial factor in tying the whole together. There is another network, not so visible, that of the service ducts, all coming together in the central Boiler House. As regards compact massing, this was, of course, achieved when one looks at the campus from a distance, as many photos here will witness. From there it is virtually impossible to distinguish out the individual parts.

Traffic Plan, 1969. In black: buildings by Lasdun which were completed by the time of his departure or shortly afterwards.
Red: pedestrian areas and walkways.
Blue: roadways.

Campus from South-East, March 1968

## THE WALKWAY SYSTEM

The University's most exclusive experience is the walkway system. It is complete, reaching to and along almost all the Lasdun buildings, with their main entrances giving out to the walkway. The 'bridges', the walkways on stilts, measure 300 m in length and are 4-8m above the ground. The remainder of the system, itself totaling over 400 m in length, is either attached to buildings, placed on top of buildings, or even leading through buildings.

Lasdun, of course, saw all this as a means to achieve the much vaunted ethos of unity of university life: 'Linkage; community, communication... encourages mixing and chance encounters'. When the latter was not happening, then 'every moment of walking is a moment of thinking.' Movement, circulation was, in fact, primary; from the outset in both Draft I and Draft II plans all pedestrian routes ran into an 'urban' square located next to and connecting all routes to the 'harbour'. (see illustrations of models on pp 69 and 83).

There is a logic in the relation of the walkway to the site: the main entrance to the system begins on flat ground; then, as the ground slopes down steeply, the pedestrian way begins to 'lift off'. Naturally, it reaches its greatest height at the far end, attached to Norfolk Terrace. Lasdun thus introduces a play of the horizontals of the communication levels against the slope of the site. The only drawback, in East Norfolk, might be the weather, yet, in 1969 Lasdun's meteorologists maintained that the rainfall was only 26 inches per annum and that south-western winds prevailed.

'Part of the joy of East Anglia is to walk between the buildings, experiencing the rich silhouettes and towers shifting against one another under the vast Norfolk sky with the grass hummocks rolling away slowly down the sedge banks and reeds of the River Yare. But the landscape romanticism is clearly more than a question of siting. The residences themselves are like so many artificial hills, complete with valleys, contours, pathways, stopping points, changes of level, cliff faces and rocky incidents' (William Curtis).

'One walks in the air, with as much of the building falling away beneath as towering above one, and this affords a sense of people being given priority over structures' (J.M.Richards).

It must be remembered that on the underside of the walkways are fitted the service ducts, another important element of the 'linkage'. Finally, mention must be made of the ostensibly most important purpose of the walkway system: to keep the users away from vehicular traffic. The street access network runs strictly underneath the walkways. Lasdun claims that this affords a maximum of direct vehicular access to all buildings, as well as helping to disperse parked cars (for a modest 25 % of car users) with 'ample cycle parking for the rest of the population'.

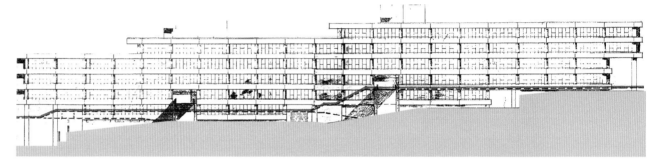

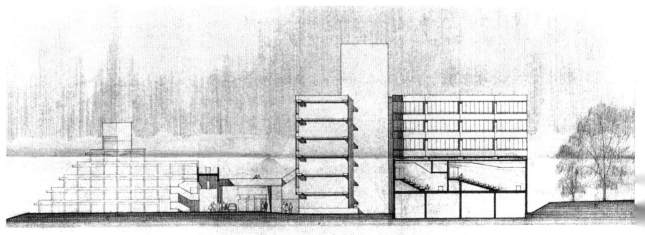

Top: Elevation of the eastern end of the Teaching Wall, indicating the way the walkway 'takes off' from ground level above the slope.

Section through 'Maths and Physics' Block (D. Lasdun, 1967, as such unbuilt), indicates relationship between teaching facilities, residences and the communication core.

Clockwise from top left: **An early photograph pointing towards the location of the section left.**

Space under the Chemistry Block; the Teaching Wall turns at a 135° angle.

Signposting, here on the car park on top of the Boiler House.

A photograph aimed at showing how UEA was meant to be used. Walkway on Suffolk Terrace. From *The Times Educational Supplement* 1968.

Alison and Peter Smithson, Competition Design for Sheffield University 1953. A prefiguration of the 1960s ideal of the 'one-building', 'urban' campus, linked by prominent pedestrian routes. (Peter Smithson on UEA: 'the Pirates of Penzance').

Encaenia, Oxford University, 1907

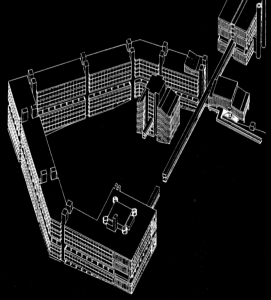

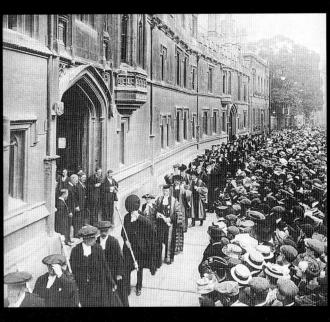

## THE TEACHING WALL

The Teaching Block is the element of Lasdun's scheme that went through a long process of change. From the complexity of main and subsidiary buildings of Draft I in early 1963 we move to the relative clarity of the huge double-spine design of Draft II later that year. The present form, the straightforward single 'spine' did not really emerge until 1966/7 and was partly the result of cuts in spending. The middle part, for the Schools of 'Maths and Physics' and Environmental Sciences was completed only in 1973 after Lasdun's departure (by David Luckhurst under Bernard Feilden), though the exterior essentially kept to Lasdun's designs. The enormous length of the 'Teaching Wall', some 460 metres, makes it a singular kind of building. Like the walkway system, the building follows, quite literally, the ethos of unity. The rigorous form of the building also has the effect that there are no untidy back yards; there are only two faces to the building, neither of which can be properly labelled 'front', or 'back - except for the fact that the main entrances off the walkway are placed on the southern side. There is only one basic principle of allocating the schools: arts are placed in the eastern end, closer to the Library, the science schools at the western end. A further declared virtue of this 'spine' system of plan was its extendibility.

It was a bold stoke to create the 'continuous teaching environment', as the American critic, Richard Dober, called it, to accommodate all teaching and research in the same kind of building - with the same ceiling height of 11', or 3.35m, floor to floor, for both arts and sciences - although some of the sciences have a few ground floor excrescences for larger laboratories. Only Essex took such a radical step away from the traditional, individual and differentiated - blocks - plan of a university (but it remained less consistent: soon after construction had begun, a lower ceiling height for arts schools was introduced). The problem, of course, remains as to whether this complete visual fusion helps with the desired identification of the users with 'their' 'Schools of Studies'; the only feature that marks the School being the main entrance over a bridge from the walkway.

Like the walkway system, the teaching wall is not straight, it bends. It 'cranks' along the site at Lasdun's favourite gentle angle of 135 degrees and it also steps down in response to the slope, while being 'orchestrated' with the walkway and with the backs of the residences.

Inside the teaching wall, there are basically only three kinds of rooms, small offices with teaching space for about eight students; middle-sized seminar rooms for about twenty, larger lecture rooms and many large laboratory spaces which take up the whole of the floor. Repeatedly the University brief-makers demanded a concentration of special communal spaces within each School, but the sequence of rooms along stretched-out corridors hardly allowed for that. An important member of Lasdun's early design team was Michael Brawne.

Plan of Teaching Wall as envisaged by Lasdun 1968; the shaded parts were left out when the block was completed in 1973.

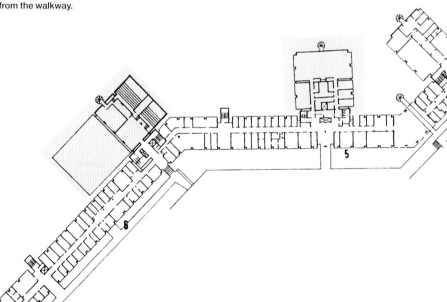

The 'backs' of Chemistry and Arts I. The central tower projection contains the lift, with machinery and also water tanks in the top compartment. The partially visible tower on the left contains a water tank, the tower on the right contains a staircase and its top is thus empty (cf. below page 87 ). – The treatment of the metal windows and sills is an expensive one: 'Kal-Colour' on Aluminium.

Below: **The Boiler House.**

## LIBRARY AND LECTURE THEATRES

Lasdun's Library was built to contain one million books and was completed in two stages (1967-8 and 1973-4). The role played by the central library in the New Universities was a very prominent one and its size was taken as a measure of the university's independence. Inside there are, in the most straightforward arrangement, six floors. However much Lasdun goes for complex spatial arrangements outside the buildings, there are no fanciful spaces inside any of his UEA buildings. Lasdun positioned the Library so that it is central, yet it is surrounded as far as possible by landscaped grounds which provides the readers with 'the greatest possible amenity' (1964 Brief). The entrance is via the walkway which, at this point, is allowed to widen out a little, to serve also as the entrance to the Lecture Theatre Block, a low, windowless box of loadbearing walls in concrete blockwork, three floors, partly dug into the ground. (1968-9, Lasdun's 'most economical building').

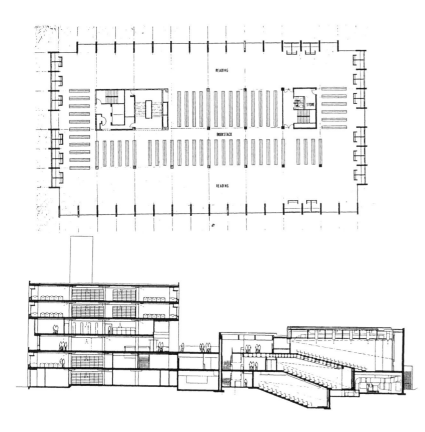

Right: **The Library from South West.**

Far left: **Plan and Section of Library and Lecture Theatres.**

Above left: **View from the Library over Suffolk Terrace and (left) over Suffolk Walk, a row of flats and maisonettes for married students and staff, 1964-7. (cf. page 73).**

Below left: **Lecture Theatre Block.**

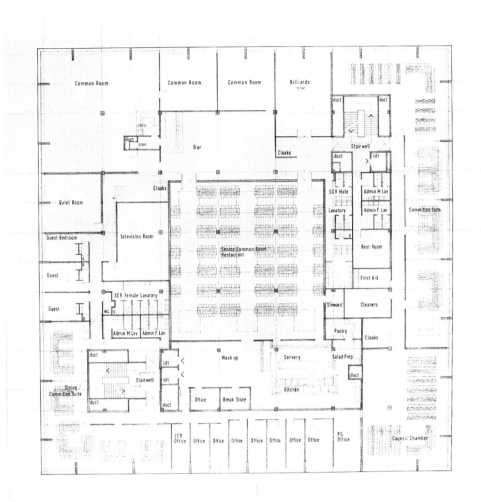

The least successful story at Lasdun's UEA is that of its central social building. This forms part of a wider set of problems concerning the social planning of the New Universities. Sussex started off by building Falmer House entirely for 'social' purposes and has never regretted it. Then, however, the collegiate universities, York, Kent, Lancaster thought they provided fully for social life in the way they organised their colleges, and thus, initially at least, did not built any central social facilities. Essex, on somewhat different grounds, also argued against such an institution. There is no element in which the New Universities vary so much as in the provision of public and semi-public spaces and buildings. UEA, from the start, did plan a large social centre (and additionally it entertained the idea of building a large public hall jointly with the City of Norwich, to be called Mackintosh Hall). In 1964 a fair-sized Students' Union was built in the Village (see pages 138-9), which happily served the university into the early 1970s.

Above left: University House, plan 1967.

Below left: University House, northern elevation.

Below: University House, western elevation.

Right: University Centre, model, c. 1966.

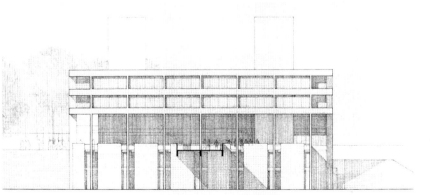

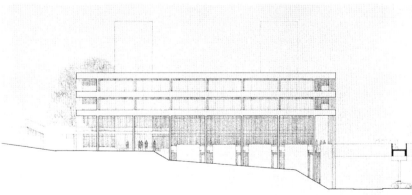

The planning process for Lasdun's central buildings suffered from two principal ills: 1) it appeared extremely difficult to determine exactly which functions should be included; 2) the growing government financial restrictions. Lasdun's plan of 1967 shown here presents a tour de force; virtually all the non-teaching functions are contained within one square box. Note the way the building was to be linked into the walkway system. 'University House' (serving mainly as the Students' Union) was completed to a greatly modified design only in 1973 (see pages 114-5).

A sub-chapter here is the issue of the Senior Common Room. Some of the Seven avoided specific reference to this kind of venue and Essex explicitly excluded it from its plans. UEA's Senior Common Room always existed institutionally, so to speak, but not always physically. It kept changing its location: from Earlham Lodge in the Village to a few rooms in University House (accessible separately from outside) to one of the mezzanines of the Sainsbury Centre and later back to the centre of the University, as the 'Top Floor', for all staff, in the Restaurant Building.

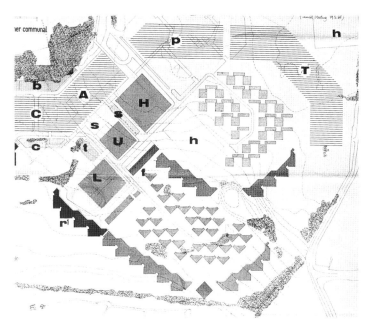

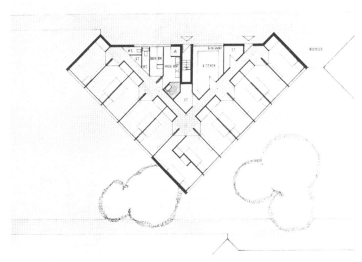

Top: Two-storey residential blocks in triangular shape and one-to-two-storey blocks around courtyards, 1967, Lasdun's economy solution.

Above: Plan of one of the triangular residential blocks.

## STUDENT RESIDENCES

UEA's best loved, or, perhaps, its most controversial buildings are the 'Ziggurats'. They are also its most complicated structures; indeed, there cannot be many examples of student residences of such a complex plan; considering that this type of building is normally treated very straightforwardly. UEA's blocks belong to the type of 'semi-A frame' or 'Terrassenhäuser' type of dwelling - to use two of the 1960s planners' and housing designers' special terms.

No plan, no section can give an idea of the true complexity. Placing blocks on edge has, first of all, a practical advantage, namely, more rooms can enjoy the view, while they are relatively free from overlooking each other. Each block also carries its own stairway at the rear angle; while the front apex is taken up by the kitchen / breakfast / common room (serving approximately 12 students). The access stairway, naturally, slopes backwards, and this corresponds to the backward slope of the building at the rear. Altogether, Lasdun's residences must be understood as a strong contrast between 'front' and 'back'. The front faces the landscape - as has been stressed, so much of UEA architecture is about enjoying the views - the back has virtually no windows at all. Behind the closed walls are the bathrooms and toilets, all artificially lit. As it was put by Lasdun's eminent colleagues, Alison and Peter Smithson (not normally known to lavish praise on the work of their contemporaries): 'Could it be that why we like Lasdun's East Anglia student clusters is because they are connective, they have a front and a back and counterpart space ...'

Entering the blocks at ground-floor level from the back means going through dark, cavernous spaces, then one meets an immensely steep and dark staircase, with its 'hole' at the top, where it leads out to the walkways. Left and right one meets the doors leading into the corridors with their exceptionally low ceilings (6' 10", or 2.08m), and finally one is virtually sucked into the blazing light of the kitchen/common room.

Two very early internal Reports of 1962 argued the succinct case of a new kind of student residence: firstly: the 'overriding need to ensure that East Anglia should develop as a community... to ensure a relationship between dons and students and among students... easy, intimate and natural... conforming to the realities of student living rather than imposing forms which might prove irksome and therefore stultifying. The weight of opinion has been... in favour of the known and tried, in the form of the collegiate system... However, financial considerations... led us to avoid even the limited collegiate solution of a... hall of residence [and to choose] a pattern of student residence with a "unitary" emphasis'. At the same time there was '... a desire to find a via media, an architectural form which would avoid the financial hazards of the collegiate arrangement and yet foster small and socially cohesive groups within an integrated community [i.e. of the university as a whole]'. 'The architectural device, the true unit of common living is the staircase... incorporated in blocks of study-bedrooms, [it] might go a long way to ensure that these [are] not mere hotels but living student communities' - and here is the explicit Oxbridge link. At the same time it must be noted that UEA's staircases are very economic in that each provides access to about sixty rooms in units of twelve. To give these ranges of buildings an element of outward identification, the architect marked each staircase block with two little towers which hold the statutory watertanks. Lasdun, furthermore, explained (in 1967) the design of the backs as 'undercrofts': 'The stepped section provides an undercroft which deals with all the backyard mess of undergraduate activities ...'

The chief idea behind the 'architectural device' of the repeated staircases was to create 'identity' and 'community'. Another notion was that of the students' 'freedom'; it was stressed frequently that they were now considered adults, there was no need for the old kinds of guidance and supervision of their lives in residence. Each corridor, as it was stressed, has 'its own front door', meaning that, once inside, the students are among themselves.

It is doubtful, however, whether Lasdun's residences also helped to do away with another notion, or convention of the old colleges and halls of residence: that of the students being 'served' by the staff. The immense contrast between front and back also meant a contrast between 'residence', and 'service' areas; the dark, always artificially lit rooms near the entrances are where the cleaners and maintenance staff congregate. As late as 1995 we read the following musings of a student user (who was straightforwardly given the task of analysing some of the salient features of UEA architecture in use): 'By [using] the suspended pedestrian walkways the students can reach various areas of the campus without ever leaving the main network of the design. This allows the maintenance staff to enter the building through the ground level without interfering with the students' ability to move around at a certain speed ...'

Some misleading comments have been made about the costs of the Ziggurats being high. The facts were that university residences were usually not financed by the government, the money for the construction had to come out of the university's own funds. The UGC nevertheless did have its cost guidelines. If a university wanted to receive moneys from the government for equipment and architect's fees, then the university had to build to UGC cost standards. UEA prided itself that the basic construction of the 684 student bedplaces was estimated at £945 each, which was the UGC limit. UEA then claimed from the UGC a further £381 for 'abnormals' (to cover what were unusual elements in the construction) and for fees and furniture, which brought the total to £1326. Very soon afterwards, UEA, like other universities, built rather cheaper (self-financing) kinds of residences (see page 120-121), but the cheapness of the Ziggurats appeared impressive when a place in a properly appointed older type of residence hall cost over £1500 and usually much more in Oxford or Cambridge. To the names of Thistlethwaite and Lasdun must be added Edward Cullinan, who worked in Lasdun's office at the time.

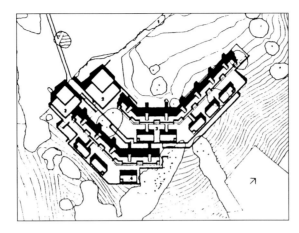

## PRECURSORS:

Top left: **Sir Leslie Martin, Royal Holloway College London, proposed student residences, c. 1960.**

Top right: **Chamberlin, Powell & Bon, proposed Hall of Residence for Birmingham University, 1960.**

Centre: **Denys Lasdun, Christ's College Cambridge Residences, section, 1966.**

Bottom: **Denys Lasdun, proposed extensions to St John's College Cambridge 1961 (Cripps Building).** 'It is sad to record that, by a narrow majority, St John's College found this scheme "somewhat too radical", but Lasdun's view is that it will bear fruit in some other form at Norwich.'

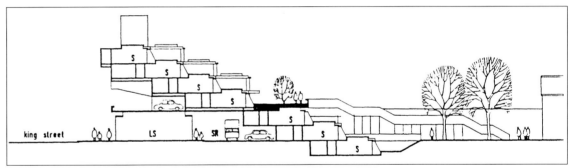

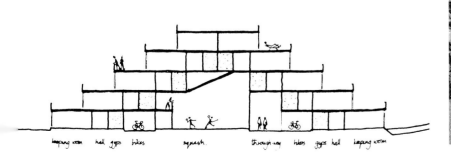

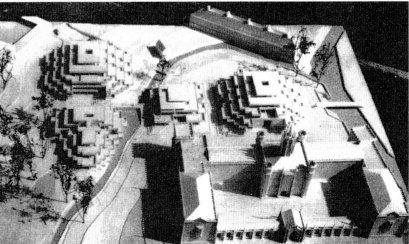

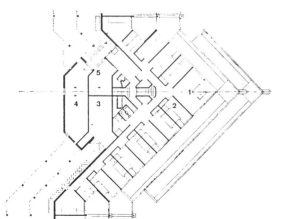

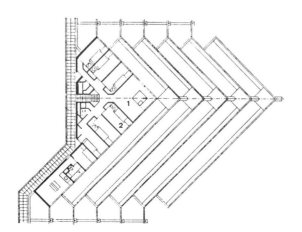

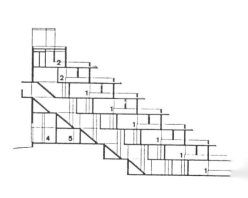

Far left: **Entrance to Suffolk Terrace.**

Left: **Back of the Residences, early photo.**

Below left: **Plans and Section.**

Above, clockwise from top left:

**Breakfast / Kitchen / Common Room.**

**Study-Bedroom.**

**Sun Terrace, photo Richard Einzig.**

**Stairs.**

Following pages:

Left: **Norfolk Terrace.**

Right: **Sports Day with Suffolk Terrace, 1970s.**

A CHANGE OF HEART

ENGLISH ARCHITECTURE SINCE THE WAR
A POLICY FOR PROTECTION

**THE ZIGGURATS: A VERSATILE IMAGE**

Top: English Heritage, *A Change of Heart*, 1992

Below right: Tony Birks's 1972 book on the New Universities.

Below left: William Curtis's 1994 monograph on Lasdun, frontispiece (photographer: Richard Einzig, c. 1969).

DENYS LASDUN
ARCHITECTURE, CITY, LANDSCAPE

WILLIAM J R CURTIS

Building
the
New Universities

Tony Birks

photographs by Michael Holford

THE NEW ENVIRONMENT    1

Top: **Sir Kenneth (Lord) Clark**, from 'Civilization', 1972, a survey history of Western Art on BBC2, last installment. Clark does not comment about the architecture as such, but the lengthy shots of the Ziggurats and of some student groups mark the end of an extraordinary sequence of events, high technology, space flight, Hiroshima etc. Clark wants to conclude his story by insisting that not all is gloom, but that there are more bright students around than ever before. He reiterates, in fact, the central ethos of the New University Movement of the early 1960s.

Top right: **Malcolm Bradbury**, 'Profile' in *Sunday Times* 1978.

Above: **Prof. Michael Thompson, Frank Whistlethwaite's** successor as Vice Chancellor (1980-86), from UEA's Prospectus 1984/5.

Right: **Students' Nightline**, Poster 1999.

Far right: **Promotional Study of the Lotus Elite**, c. 1974 (produced at Hethel, Norfolk).

# nightline
503504 · Norfolk Terrace C03.12

*Every night, one light is always on.*

**LASDUN'S SKYLINE.**

The formations of blocks on the top of Lasdun's buildings provide an opportunity to follow the Modernist game of 'form follows function', or 'form versus function'. Seen from close by or inside, the excrescences are enormous, the size of two-to four-storied buildings, hence they can be seen from a long way. They provide the vertical accents in an architecture which, basically, like most of his buildings, Lasdun intended to be 'horizontal'. It should be remembered that Lasdun, on occasions, dug out the ground in order to prevent the buildings from appearing too high.

In principle all these structures serve a practical function. The very large blocks contain special water tanks (which have to be large because scientists need water pressure to remain absolutely constant), lift machinery and ventilation mechanisms. They are placed in the position they are, centrally, because they are supported by the in situ concrete 'communication cores' of the buildings, and they are clearly shown to be supported in this way on the outside. The School of Mathematics and Physics also carries a completely exposed lecture theatre with a raked floor (see frontispiece). The corresponding blocks on the Arts Block are

much smaller because elaborate services are not needed. The blocks on top of the residences are mostly taken up by water tanks.

So far the function. Enter purely formal considerations. There seems only one excrescence completely without proper function, the top of the right-hand tower on Chemistry which is empty and just complements the tower on the left (see page 79). The use of the 'hammerhead' projection on many towers creates a little more room for the servicing of the machinery but is chiefly a feat of concrete cantilever construction, and thus, in effect, largely a formal device, introduced not long before by the New Brutalist School.

The prominent ventilation inlet for Biology, of a pronounced Corbusierian sculptural shape, differs formally, but not functionally, from the inlet for the Chemistry Block which one hardly notices. Above all, there is no strictly practical need to expose all these parts to the extent they are, on the exterior. Lasdun called it 'the theme of vertical circulation cores, terminating on the skyline, with concrete roof structures'. I will make a feature of services and stacks on top of the buildings' – 'theme', 'feature' of course being the perfect words to fudge the form vs. function issue and 'circulation' being one of the keys to Lasdun's architectural rhetoric explained in this chapter.

# Denys Lasdun: Rhetoric in Words, Models, Photographs and Reinforced Concrete

The analysis of the process of patronage and the practical description of a building, be they ever so detailed, are not sufficient for the understanding of a work of architecture as a whole. Some would even maintain that too close a focus on either may result in missing the point of good architecture altogether. What is it that we need in addition to detail; what do we call that which is held to be the essential in architecture? In traditional architecture the answer seemed simple: dignity and beauty. A university is a building of very high institutional importance, only a church, a ruler's palace and perhaps a big city hall are of higher public rank. By means of distinguishing size, formal composition and a great amount of decoration, the patron and the designer tried to give architectural distinction to such an institution. In brief, a university is expected to present a striking and beautiful building. But can these categories still be applied to a Modernist building? The Modernists themselves, of the early to mid-twentieth century, usually avoided a direct answer, but very few of them would give a straight no. This could certainly be a summary of the many comments on the Sainsbury Centre cited above. The more recent Postmodernist interpretation of Modernism tends to stress the traditional ways of thinking in twentieth century architecture. Modernist designers, as always, went for the big and often the massive. They did not try and question, at least until the 1960s, the old hierarchy of public buildings. While not normally thinking in terms of ornament, Modernists devised patterns and colour schemes which they wanted to be effective in purely visual-formal terms.

How does Lasdun's mature work fit in here? William Curtis, to whom we owe major monographs of the architect's work, tends to stress what he sees as the 'eternal' qualities of Lasdun's work and does not abstain from traditional epithets, especially 'monumental'. Lasdun himself, however, appears to try to avoid many of these kinds of traditional terms. On the other hand, Lasdun is one of those architects who hold forth a great deal about their own buildings and who are eager for their users to listen to what they have to say. One of the postmodern ways to avoid any firm definitions of what is 'essential' in architecture is to tackle the whole problem under the heading of language. What we are concerned with here is a discourse on architecture, something which somehow exists both separately alongside the actual building, but is also intimately linked to it. Here our special angle is the language of praise. Hence the term rhetoric has been chosen. It, too, needs an apology. Modernists did not like the old term rhetoric; if anything, it served, for them, to characterise what could be bad, or superfluous. Today, however, we consider rhetoric as something normal again, or at least we have to admit that it occurs practically everywhere, not least in all the statements which a university makes about itself. Rhetoric, in this chapter, is treated as an art form in itself, which we may try to analyse to help us with our understanding of the university's architecture.

When we briefly introduced the planning of the Seven English New Universities we referred to the particular way in which all patrons and designers perceived a unity of architectural form and social purpose. We may here use a term found in a Canadian architectural journal of 1962: 'social form'. It is meant there to provide a general characterisation of Post-War English architecture, and in particular of Lasdun's designs. The journal maintains that the chief problem lies in the separation between architects' architecture, the artistic individuality of their designs, on the one hand, and the purely economic, utilitarian and social aims of architecture, on the other. Lasdun is seen as one of the few designers who unites both spheres successfully. We may, again, here try to understand the problem chiefly in terms of language. Within the discourse of Welfare State social reform there were two strands: the mundane one of professional technological progress, and the more general and rhetorical one of heightened social and moral reform ethos. What the Canadian article does not recognise is that there had been a long tradition, going back into the nineteenth century, a conviction that artistic ethos and social aims must and can be fused in the language of all pronouncements. For most architectural protagonists, such as Le Corbusier, Gropius, as well as for many of the British Welfare State architects of the 1950s and 1960s, it was essential to overcome these divisions between socio-psychological ideas of living and architectural art. In fact the unity of all factors was the essence of the utopian projects and the utopianist language in architecture and town planning.

But the utopias varied from architect to architect, or, in the new university institutions, from one architect/vice-chancellor team to the next. At Sussex we meet what was essentially a pre-Modernist understanding of architectural quality. Thus Basil Spence, its architect: 'the level of aesthetic appreciation usually marks the standard of achievement of a civilisation'. The simple and most immediate result of the architect's approach was increased expense. Similar statements can be found at Warwick, Kent and even York, although for the latter campus the words 'beauty' and 'monumentality' were seemingly banned by the architects, even though in the end the highest architectural aim was to look like the Cambridge Backs. At Essex one occasionally heard strong statements about the uncompromising nature of its architecture while Lancaster chose to avoid rhetoric altogether.

# RIBA GOLD FOR LASDUN

Sir Denys Lasdun has been awarded the Royal Gold Medal for Architecture, 1977. The citation speaks of "a body of work which has rightly earned him both national and international praise and respect" and of "an architectural development and concern for quality and detail which Lasdun, his

'There is a thing called gut reaction in architecture'

partners, colleagues and patrons, have consistently striven for".

"At a time when we are right to encourage the virtues of preservation and gentle renewal," it concludes, "we are right too to recognise that we need artists who can give us new things to enjoy. Of such artists, Lasdun is one of the distinguished few."

Denys Lasdun has long been held in high regard by his professional peers but last year, with the publicity surrounding the opening of the National Theatre, his name became more widely known. Despite the current public disaffection for modern architecture, his reputation has survived and gone from strength to strength.

Lasdun has always stuck steadfastly to the principles of the Modern Movement and is not afraid to acknowledge the influence of Le Corbusier whose reputation is currently at its lowest ebb. In an interview with *Building* last year he spoke of the impact of the publication in 1927 of a translation of *Vers une Architecture:* "I read it from cover to cover more than once and I went to Paris almost immediately . . . I found Le Corbusier's Pavillion Suisse stunning."

As Royal Gold Medallist Lasdun joins most of the big names of the Modern Movement, including Le Corbusier himself who received the medal in 1953. Auguste Perret received it in 1948, Alvar Aalto in 1957 and Mies van der Rohe in 1959. Maxwell Fry, the Modern Movement's English pioneer, for whom Lasdun worked for a short time in the early fifties (while Fry in turn was working for Le Corbusier in Chandigarh) got his gold medal in 1964.

The Gold Medal is not necessarily awarded to practising architects. It was instituted in 1848 by Queen Victoria and is conferred annually by the Sovereign on "some distinguished architect or group of architects, for work of high merit or on some distinguished person or persons whose work has promoted, either directly or indirectly the advancement of architecture."

'It is earthbound architecture that I am interested in'

Non-architect medal winners have included historians (Sir John Summerson, Nikolas Pevsner and Lewis Mumford) theorists (Buckminster Fuller) and engineers (Ove Arup and Pier Luigi Nervi).

This year's Royal Gold Medal jury was chaired by Eric Lyons who will make the formal presentation to Lasdun at a special ceremony at the RIBA headquarters on 28 June.

Lasdun at the height of his career; he was knighted in 1976.

Top left: *Lasdun's first building – a house at Paddington, 1938.*
Far left: *Cluster block at Bethnal Green, 1955.*
Middle left: *Flats in St James's Place, 1958.*
Middle top: *The University of London, designed in 1965.*
Above: *University of East Anglia, 1968 – reflecting the idea of "earthbound architecture".*
Left: *The National Theatre, opened last year, which finally set the seal on Lasdun's reputation.*

One of the most ambitious architectural rhetoricians was Denys Lasdun. In many ways like Le Corbusier, Lasdun was a compulsive proseletyser, who, from the late 1950s, simply had to accompany his designs with a kind of running commentary, embroidering it with frequent apercus about world architecture, society and life in general. These comments seemed eminently quotable. Whenever a building of his was dealt with in a periodical or a book, one could read Lasdun's characteristic language. Lasdun was not an architectural theoretician of note, nor did he write on more technical matters, and he very rarely engaged with the professional polemics of the day. One simply has to remember the most ancient function of rhetoric: Lasdun, in Frank Thistlethwaite's words, was 'marvellous at exposition'. To an extent the architect became the spokesperson for the University as a whole, the public relations agent of UEA in its most important early years. As we have witnessed, Lasdun was most intensely concerned with the way his work, and with the way he himself, as a practitioner, was presented. When he left UEA, it was less the fact of his leaving that concerned him, than the ways in which this fact was publicised. On the whole, Lasdun succeeded in giving an impression that he 'talks with great conviction and passion of the things he really believes in' *(The Times)*. This could, however, also result in adverse remarks: 'Patrons and committees manage to swallow the polemical idealism whole, only to find the concrete artefact somewhat indigestible' *(Spectator)*.

Lasdun took the 'architect as briefmaker' position further than many others. His most impressive, most notorious and most often repeated statement was that about the client who does not know what he or she wants, but in the end accepts the architect's solution as the one he had 'always wanted'. Thus Lasdun felt he had a comprehensive view of the University's needs. He even saw it as his task, occasionally, to comment on the teaching programme itself, for instance, about the 'academic growing points at interstices between established disciplines', and he assures us that his Teaching Wall 'can cope with disciplines not yet known'. Not only does Lasdun assume the role of the briefmaker, he is even liable to claim, as in the case of the National Theatre, that he had no prior experience with that type of building and that therefore he would start with basics. His art 'takes in the whole of human experience'. At UEA, in 1963, he began with 'three criteria': 'a sense of place; a sense of people, a sense of time'. He also frequently spoke more simply of the 'poetics of architecture', of 'form in light', of 'sculpture' and of 'space': 'architecture expresses itself primarily through the quintessential medium of space'. These statements, of course, were standard Modernist practice.

But there was another kind of language which was more specific and more novel. Here Lasdun was indebted to some extent (although he denies it) to Alison and Peter Smithson and their socio-psychological terminology of 'human association' and 'human action', as well as to the American writer on town design, Kevin Lynch. Buildings and their functions are not considered in a contemplative mood (as in the case of Spence), but actively and dynamically. This impression of activity and movement, in its apparently spontaneous multidirectionality, is opposed to that of the static rectangularity of earlier Modernism; the new key word, 'antidiagrammatic', has been mentioned several times in our descriptions. But Lasdun's metaphors are usually quite specific in their application to his buildings, while the Smithsons applied their rhetoric chiefly to their illustrations and sketches and their efforts largely remained on paper. Some of the Smithson/Lasdun terms are topological-geographical, or geological, such as 'concentration', 'cluster', 'linkage', 'strata', or 'cascading', 'landlocked harbour'; UEA was to be the 'architecture of urban landscape'. Lasdun thus made notable contributions to the 'genius loci' rhetoric. On other occasions Lasdun uses terms taken from physics or biology, such as 'nucleus', 'spine', 'circuit', though he does not strain the term 'organic' used by many other Modernist designers of the time (for example, Alvar Aalto) who were pursuing somewhat similar aims. There are, in fact, very few properly 'organic' curved forms in Lasdun's architecture.

What is most notable, perhaps, is that Lasdun does not praise his buildings, like Spence, by referring to the presence, or the necessity of art and aesthetics, and he rarely uses other common terms of general architectural praise, such as 'beautiful', or 'monumental', nor do we meet comments that point in the direction of the Picturesque, as at York. It would appear that Lasdun was not specially worried with the colour of his concrete (York's great concern). In short, Lasdun did not really care for 'art' on the campus; literally, Lasdun lacked interest in outdoor sculpture, or even in lavish interior design, in contrast to most other new campuses which availed themselves of some 'extras', of works of Modernist fine art. On the contrary, Lasdun on occasions tried to transfer monies from fittings to buildings. Neither does Lasdun normally refer to any purely material and economic factors or achievements in his buildings. Not surprisingly, there is no stress - in contrast, again, to York - on the economic performance of his architecture.

What Lasdun attempts is to pinpoint the actual use of the building, the way users behave, or rather, he tries to combine the description of the buildings' form with the specifics of their use. He operates with all kinds of words, words that are general and specific, essentialist and metaphorical. These elements of use are mostly not those of a mundane, but also of a somehow heightened, special existence. Lasdun calls the University 'a map of social relationships'; or, on the walkways 'every moment of walking is a moment of thinking'.

Lasdun's was an architectural planning and an architectural rhetoric of a special kind. While it would be difficult in most Modern buildings of that date to identify parts that may be called ornament (at Sussex this is arguable), it was still customary to provide special accents for the more honorific parts of a building, by placing entrances symmetically, for instance at the Libraries of Kent and Warwick. Oth-

Denys Lasdun, European Investment Bank, Luxembourg, 1973, detail of entrance foyer, showing the continuity of the treatment of reinforced concrete inside and out.

ers, like Le Corbusier, imbued with a sense of the 'myth of man' and other poetic ideas, tended to attach, or place next to their buildings, enigmatic symbols, such as sculptures or murals. In the post-Lasdun buildings at UEA, under Feilden and Luckhurst, we shall observe a return to the older architectural concepts of decorum. But Lasdun, like Louis Kahn or Capon at Essex, knows no hierarchy of decorum. There is nothing that can be called attached art or ornament. Lasdun does not wish to differentiate between zones with a primarily decorative or symbolic character, as being opposed to those of a primarily utilitarian character. There is no axiality, no symmetry, no facade of any kind, no general contrast between 'front' and 'back'. There is no real centre, no very obvious 'entrance' to the campus; plan and form appear 'continuous'. No wonder that this radical kind of design appeared perplexing, even confusing to some. Even more than at UEA, we can observe Lasdun's rejection of customary thinking at the National Theatre, a building type which carries a strong traditional division between honorific and utilitarian parts. Here, reinforced concrete serves as the chief unifying element. The National Theatre shows virtually the same treatment of concrete throughout, back and front, inside and out. At UEA there are some differences of treatment between site-cast and pre-cast elements; but here, too, a grey solidity rules throughout. To some of his contemporaries in the 1960s concrete meant the possibility of lavish curves in architecture (Jørn Utzon in his Sydney Opera House); to Lasdun concrete only meant hard edges. Highly individualised as the design appears as a whole, it is made up of only a limited number of repeated parts.

What has so frequently been misunderstood about Lasdun's most controversial parts of UEA, the backs of the Ziggurats, must also be seen as a case of deliberate rhetorical heightening. Lasdun: 'the stepped section provides an undercroft which deals with all the backyard mess of undergraduate activities ...'; the design and the impression of these areas is perhaps greyer and darker, 'messier', than it needed to be; but this must be experienced in contrast with the blazing light and greenery, once the 'flats' are entered. It is the rhetoric of a heightened experience, but the heightened experience of ordinary use. All parts of Lasdun's buildings appear actively antidiagrammatic, agitated even, in analogy to the movements of the users, as desired by the architect. The rhetoric, if our term can be stretched that far, goes right through.

While there might be intrinsic problems in relating verbal rhetoric to built form, there are none as regards the relationship between buildings and illustrations of buildings. The way we see, understand and remember Modernist architecture is closely linked with the rhetorical methods in which the designers guide our eyes, by means of enhanced drawings, models and photographs. As the New Universities were undertakings of a somewhat unpredictable pace of growth and because of the complexities of the plans and shapes, drawings and models played a massively important role in the initial presentations,

# THE CAMERAMAN

Richard Einzig, the "architect's photographer", sets out to capture a building in the way the designer first envisaged it to look.

Above: **Richard Einzig at UEA (c.1969).**

Below:**Back of the Ziggurats, photograph by Richard Einzig; an effective image, which, however, offers no real explanation of the building.**

for the buildings as well as for the institution as a whole. For York, the diagrams of the Development Plan were the most significant visual announcements. At Sussex, Spence's drawings played a greater role; in their heavy, sometimes almost Piranesian picturequesness they followed the new mood in English architectural drawing of the 1950s, inspired by the Townscape movement. On the whole, though, Brighton attracted more attention with the finished buildings than with its plans. For Essex, on the other hand, the giant model of late 1963, endlessly reproduced, remained the chief image of the institution for a long time.

There can be few Modernist architects for whom the model played such an important role as for Denys Lasdun. In 1964 a modelmaker, Philip I. Wood, actually joined the firm. Lasdun's models are usually of balsa wood only, without the many illusionistic tricks Modernist modelmaking is capable of. His models were, first of all, essential in the design process, and Lasdun was well known for the length of time it took him to arrive at the final version of the form. The advantages of the model over a drawing or a perspective as a means to show what the buildings will be like are obvious; yet Lasdun's models develop a character of their own. The grain of the wood, the fact that it is left unpainted, gives the models a degree of unity and the character of a homogenous sculpture. Of course, these are exactly those elements which Lasdun considered intrinsic to his architecture, especially where it consists of impenetrable concrete blocks. Finally, as few people actually see the models, what really matters are the photographs of the models. These were, in turn, heavily manipulated by the angle of the light. Lasdun made sure that this was done by his specialist architectural photographers. We thus perceive the building through two layers of rhetoric, the model and the photograph of the model. In April 1963 Lasdun presented the seemingly huge (in reality quite small) model of 'Draft I' of UEA, accompanied by a special model of the residences and only one very schematic, rather un-visual plan of the whole. Photos of these models were reproduced in innumerable publications and all analyses of the buildings, such as Brett's seemingly deep appreciation, quoted above, were made from the models or the photographs of the models. Later these were succeeded by a series of top professional photographs of the 'completed' campus which the firm undertook in order to supply the journals, culminating in the lavish spread in *Architectural Design* in 1969. Yet even these accounts still include 'night' photographs of the models which Lasdun kept updating during the building campaign.

But here we have clearly reached a point when rhetoric can become dangerous; the impressiveness of Lasdun's pictorial presentation in 1969 may have diverted attention away from the state of incompleteness on the ground. The problem with rhetoric is that it is never guaranteed to 'work'.

Right: **Model of the Chemistry Block and the Library, c. 1966/7, used in architectural journals as late as 1969.**

Opposite: **Model of an early version of the Residences, colour slide of c. 1963.**

# 1968 and after: Disillusionment and Consolidation

The next chapter in UEA's history can be taken as a demonstration of the way in which negative rhetoric can be just as effective as praise. Almost contemporary with the grand photographic displays came the disappointments. It was too obvious that the reality was slow and patchy in coming on, at East Anglia, while the eventual reality at Essex appeared diminutive when compared with the grandiose intentions of 1963. This new mood coincided with a general scepticism concerning comprehensive architectural and social/sociological programmes. Modernist architecture was now taking a new turn with a new, radical emphasis on the factual, the practical, supposedly taking the users' point of view. The early 1960s dream of building a campus university as an ideal town now appeared futile. The architectural change went in tandem with a changeover from paternalist to more liberal attitudes in educational philosophy. The historical complication of the New Universities was that they straddled both phases; especially at Essex, where we find the beginnings of a freer educational outlook combined with a highly determinist plan.

The crisis of 1968 was one of those events about which one wonders, afterwards, what it was all about. From a later perspective it appears puzzling that there was virtually never any criticism of the universities' performance in purely academic terms. What matters here was the way in which the New Universities, in particular, seemed to have gone wrong. 'Dream exposed as sham', 'beyond redemption'... 'shut Essex'. The case of Essex was the most severe, and, true to that institution, the most publicised. Rumours later on even hinted at the closure of some of the New Universities: 'Kent, Aston, Lancaster and East Anglia ...; privately, students, officials and lecturers at other universities add the names Essex and Warwick ....' (1977). Sceptics could argue that after the hype, a fall was inevitable; the self congratulatory language of the universities' spokespersons would soon be matched by ultra critical language of the journalist-investigators, such as Michael Beloff, Tony Birks, John Maule McKean and

Peter Wilby - whose insights are, in themselves, admirable pieces of analysis.

The story of the actual 'events' has been told many times. It meant, above all, for the New Universities that they found themselves suddenly, and unexpectedly, hosting a new kind of person: the 'New Student'. From the idea of a community of paternalistic benevolent dependence and benign rule, educational philosophy had moved, during the 1960s, to a concept of community in which there was more of a feeling of equality. The anti-paternalist New Student thus did follow in a line of development that had already begun before international Student Power arrived. By 1968 this development had been propelled forward to a point at which not only the older paternalistic model but also the newer liberal model was rejected. At the same time teachers found that the high hopes of flexible interdisciplinary teaching had not been fulfilled. Wilby roundly declared that Asa Brigg's famous project of 'redrawing the map of learning' had 'without doubt failed'. There had been experiments but no innovations. By 1968, the new universities' founding (and funding) body, the UGC, had long gone off experiments and was almost exclusively concerned with numbers, by increasing student places in existing older institutions.

Whatever went wrong, any incompleteness or inconsistency, the blame was always put on the university as a whole, on the institution, and this even included the bad weather. According to Birks it rains on more than 200 days a year in Lasdun's UEA. The notion of the 'total university community', as formulated by at least six of the Seven, seemed elusive. To those who have studied other provisions of the Welfare State this comes as no surprise. In housing, sociologists who had earlier been propagating 'community' most fervently, now announced, on the basis of 'intensive empirical investigation', that they could not give recipes as to how effective communities could be designed. Likewise, in the universities, 'that nirvana of staff-student integration ...'... 'the idea of a single institution was a myth that existed only in Asa Briggs's mind' (Wilby). Much blame was put here also on staff who did not fulfil their side of avoiding the '9-5 university'.

More importantly in our context, 'failure' was not only blamed on the institution, but on its architecture. One has to remember that severe criticism of recently erected buildings and putting the blame on them for a wide range of personal and social ills is a very common phenomenon. Such a criticism compounds lesser, or at least more accidental failures of building quality, such as a leaking roof, with more fundamental perceived ills. What appeared so fateful in that criticism, certainly in England, was the way in which failure was not blamed on indifference in design, but on the contrary, it was directed at the 'highly designed' campuses, such as East Anglia or Essex. The latter's 'failings' 'represented not too little thought and imagination, it represented too much of it.'

A nasty remark by Beloff was aimed at finally demolishing any socio-urban reputation of the new universities: 'Only cemeteries are sited as far out of towns as the universities'. Universities should prefe ably be situated inside the town. The demand, made in Norwich in 1960, to place the university in th city centre was dug up again; it was now held that the actual space occupied by the buildings of UE, namely 75 acres, corresponded exactly to the proposed city site (see page 142). The most favourab conclusion which the new universities could hope for in the early to mid-seventies was that there wa not that much difference between them and 'the rest'; '...some assume that in the New Universities ever thing may be made anew each year...', Thistlethwaite wrote defensively as early as 1968. '...They a not as distinctive as all that'. Indeed, soon the students were to quieten down and the journalist-inve: tigators to tone down their exaggerations and the vice-chancellors had to swallow some of their prid too. Thirty years later, most buildings still function much the same way they were originally intended t even science buildings. In the end, there was nothing in the events of 1968-74 which really prejudice either the academic quality, or the ultimate architectural merits of the Seven.

## A PORTION OF TROUBLE.  MIXED USER REACTIONS

A league table of New University troubles and the ensuing national publicity would not be difficult to estal lish. Ranging far behind Essex as regards depth and frequency, and behind Warwick, too, as regarc seriousness, UEA probably came third, ahead of Sussex. According to Wilby, UEA's troubles had n been as 'prolonged and self-destructive' as those of other universities. On the other hand, UEA did expe rience serious problems, not least because of the way, to quote Wilby again, it felt 'highly self-consciou and self critical'. In May 1968, student activists at UEA had regretted the 'lack of fire among' undergraduate in comparison to Essex. Indeed, the protests, the first incidents and demonstrations developed out student pranks and appeared spontaneous. In 1968 Princess Margaret had to witness the unsuc cessful burning of a cardboard carrier, bearing a Union Jack, and shouts of 'Vietnam Murderer'. The real severe troubles, break-ins, sit-ins and strikes came in late 1970 and early 1971 as a result of the appa ent mismanagement of drug cases, culminating in a student break-in to search for files on studer informers. Town-and-gown relationships, as elsewhere, sharply deteriorated. After the Princess Ma garet incident Norwich landladies were quoted by the newspapers as saying: 'We quit!' 'No mor students!' In any case, the townspeople seemed to have little awareness of their university; by 196( 34 % did not know where the University was and only 25 % had ever been there, a disappointing resu after all the local efforts and the continuous support from the local press.

The assessment of UEA architecture around 1968-1972 is a complex matter. Lasdun's Univers ty ranged somewhere between Sussex whose architecture was seldom criticised and the buildings a ssex which were condemned outright. During 1968-70, Lasdun's UEA was the subject of extensive architect-inspired praise in professional architectural journals, national and world-wide. From then onwards the Ziggurats emerged as a standard image for new universities in a much wider range of publications, and while the buildings were not necessarily called beautiful, they certainly seemed intriguing and memorable.

This is the image, or part of the image, as perceived from outside. The reactions of the users, were, likewise, subject to fluctuations. It appears that the first cohort of undergraduates in Lasdun's teaching blocks and the residences in 1968-70 still belonged to a pre-1968 university world: 'We enjoyed being students... not many responsibilities... do what you want... proud of the university ...'. There were many comments about the novelty of subject combinations and the effectiveness of teaching. 'A three year intellectual gang-bang.' 'A self-conscious newness'. These feelings seemed, in turn, strongly linked to the architectural forms: 'all new, modern, different, exciting... not Redbrick... Norfolk and Suffolk, when the lights were off, like battleships going to the river... magnificent'; 'we all knew the name of Lasdun...'. It did not seem to matter too much at that time that the buildings also appeared 'stark... the walkways cold', that the landscaping still had to be done. There was a belief on the part of the teachers that students shared their enthusiasm: 'The Students feel that the experiment needs their interest and their enthusiasm'. And yet, it would be wrong to expect too many students to trouble much over the finer points of the designer's and the critic's stipulations; there was 'simply too much else going on'. From the staff, notably from the older members, praise would be harder to expect. 'A building for a university should show dignity and grace' was a comment heard from those with a pre-Modernist architectural outlook. On a more superficial level of appreciation there were many who simply 'hated the concrete'. It would probably be fair to say that the majority of those who visited UEA disliked concrete *per se*.

It soon appeared inevitable, that Lasdun's architecture would be drawn into the pervasive discourse of criticism of these years. The simple fact of non-completion on University Plain loomed large. When the architectural journals made a decision to report on the occasion of the completion of 'Stage I' – they acted practically as mouthpieces of Lasdun's office. Unlike other types of buildings, such as theatres or museums, new universities could, by their very nature, rarely be considered complete; there was never a real 'opening' which could occasion a full assessment of their initial functioning and meaning. UEA, i.e. Lasdun's 'University Plain' was, in fact, by 1970, the least complete of all the Seven. To the new group of journalist-investigators of those years, such as Beloff and Birks, these facts could not be hidden. To the latter, UEA seemed 'like a dinosaur expiring with the disappearance of the staple diet.'

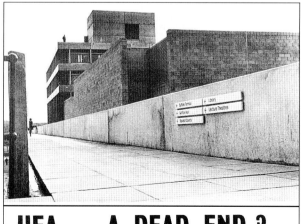

# UEA — A DEAD END ?

Above: Students leaving the Arts Block, after occupation and marching to Earlham Hall, 17 March 1971

Left: The title of an article in the UEA Student Magazine *Mandate* in late 1969.

Right: Photos of students at the University often reveal the way in which the authorities want to see them. To begin with, very few photographs occur of this 'motif' in the 1960s. The photo of the students in the newly-opened Residences (top left): was published locally (*EDP* 1966).

Much the same location, but a totally different image of the students, (*The Times* 1971).

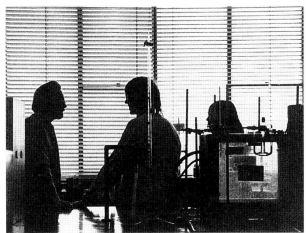

Below: From the 1970s University publicity regularly included pictures of the campus 'in use'. But both servility and rebellion are excluded. All now seems enjoyable; a dutiful, as well as a free university life. (From the Undergraduate Prospectus of 1977).

This is the first of a series of occasional photographs of life at universities in Britain. The four casually dressed students above re relaxing on the terrace of one of the blocks of study-bedrooms at East Anglia University. Opened in October, 1963, it was one f the seven new universities built during the expansion programme of the sixties.

Already by late 1968 Council felt compelled to investigate feelings on the campus and produc an internal report. By 1969 the heavy architectural sociology-speak of those years was voiced by som mature students at UEA, too, encouraged especially by Nick Zurbrugg of English and American Stu ies in the Student Magazine, *Mandate*. '...Lasdun's buildings... a dream, socially and educationally nightmare'. They 'contribute to all that is negative at the university'. There was, as one would almo expect to hear, 'a failure of community'... the 'failure' of UEA 'to effectively establish a genuine patte of integrated learning has produced a failure of community and vice-versa.' [1]

In 1972 Lasdun's UEA became the subject of a close analysis in the *Architects' Journal*, thoug it was far less incisive than that of Essex which was to appear shortly later. It concentrated much on th student troubles and the worsening town-and-gown relations, and the blame for this was put explic ly on the choice of the isolated site and on some elements of the architecture. The *Architects' Journ* repeated the by now familiar criticism of the inherently incomplete 'urban' and community concept a campus university. When it comes to planning and building details, there are actually few major cri cisms, the main one being lack of parking spaces. 'Lasdun seriously underestimated car parkir facilities'. This became an ever recurrent issue at UEA. Already by 1967/8 the Vice Chancellor was co templating fees. [2]

Looking back after many decades and bearing in mind that in 1971 we are at the nadir of the Ne Universities' reputation generally, somebody had to undertake fundamental criticisms of UEA. It was ty ical for those years that Birks, although he praised UEA in 'pure' design terms, nevertheless preferre Lancaster, precisely because of its apparent lack of architectural individuality. Birks put the chief prol lems of Lasdun's campus plainly: an overlarge plan, financial cut-backs and an unsatisfactory syste of building priorities. The second, equally important, though far less documented reason, was that f most staff at UEA the continuing use of the cosy 'village', which even by 1971 still contained the ma social facilities, was a hindrance for the recognition of Lasdun's work.

1. Further from Mandate: 'In many important ways the architectural shapes condition our experience at UEA. It is significant, for example, that the Arts/Chemistry Block is referred to by the authorities as the 'Teaching Wall'. It's a wall that we are up against, a wall with all the implications of partition and separation.... The second floor of the Arts Block has become an informal area, where, in theory, faculty and students mingle: in fact is nothing more than a standard teaching accommodation emptied of standard teaching equipment. The paper cup slum is a good reason on its own for mass absenteeism.... It is the result of a basic flaw in the design of UEA... a failure to recognise that people need and desire to live an integrated life ...'. 'The existing University structure on the Plain inhibits, rather than encourages. It lacks the qualities of freedom, variety and sympathy essential to social intercourse.' 'The strange kind of plan of Lasdun's movement, connecting parts which did not need connecting; th ground was not to be touched.'. 'The Village on the other hand seemed free... a comfortab pleasurable atmosphere.' The author, Robert Haynes was a student of art history who ha previously studied architecture at the Architectural Association.

Cf. also The Guardian 1971: 'Bad campus plan, no focal point in this community - ge eration gap... outdated... and an authoritarian administrative structure'.

2. The 1972 *AJ* Report: Upjohn/Crawshaw are critical particularly of Lasdun's access pa tern: 'Unresolved confusion of traffic and pedestrian circulation; no approach, no entrance [Lasdun had planned a prominent bus turnaround in front of the Arts II portico, but th

# BERNARD FEILDEN'S AND DAVID LUCKHURST'S COMPLETION OF LASDUN'S UEA

By the end of 1968 UEA saw itself in many ways thrown back to the early days of its existence. It had to look for a planner and designer. Having had to grapple with years of Lasdun's distant management of UEA design, it appeared plausible to engage a local firm. The Norwich practice of Feilden & Mawson offered itself for a great number of reasons. It stood for quick efficient work, not only in the 'Village' but also at the Research Park at Colney nearby. Meanwhile its senior partner had gained considerably in stature as a restorer of cathedrals and could hardly be called a 'local' architect any more. Feilden's handling of the take-over was fully adequate to the delicacy of the situation. When Thistlethwaite first approached him, during November 1968, and told him about Lasdun's imminent departure, Feilden uttered his 'profound dismay' and called it a 'major tragedy'. In fact he sounded more disappointed than the client.

But he did not hesitate to accept the invitation to become the Consultant Architect, out of loyalty to Norwich and loyalty to Frank Thistlethwaite whose architectural acumen he greatly respected. He told the Vice Chancellor that he intended to 'retrieve something from the wreck' even though it was a 'thankless task'. In spite of all the difficulties, Feilden felt a great loyalty to Lasdun's work. This was because of his general modesty and his reverence for a 'great architect'. 'I admire Lasdun as an architect. My values are not as well defined as his. I am more pragmatic. I am a team person rather than an egoist ...'. He was keen to go and see Lasdun - and Lasdun, on his part, did not mind helping him. Feilden thus provided the final support in the process of smoothing Lasdun's departure, to the benefit of all involved.

In fact, Lasdun remained one of the project architects under Feilden. Arts II was completed during 1970. Maths & Physics as well Environmental Sciences, the missing link of the Teaching Wall, were finished after some hesitation, in 1973, and the Library in 1974. This virtually completed the first phase of Lasdun's UEA. Feilden took care to adhere to Lasdun's landscape concept, and this meant chiefly not to build on those grounds which Lasdun stipulated as landscape surroundings. Under Feilden, the

*Mr. Bernard Feilden and one of his assistants, Mr. David Luckhurst, looking at a plan of the University of East Anglia last night.*

**Bernard Feilden and David Luckhurst in 1969.**

was abandoned when the county planners insisted on a one-way road system; information Peter Yorke]. There is also outright criticism of the backs of Lasdun's residences: parking there was full. 'It has proved in practice not so much a way of getting rid of backyards as of creating them. The stained car-strewn alleys are the most depressing places in the university. This was not for the abuse by the users, but how it was always meant to be'. Feilden put in plants and creepers. – 'The Lasdun buildings treat the ground as a foreign element'. The analysis in the *AJ* broadly also concurs with the students' criticism of the years before: schools have not developed as the social centres they were meant to form; the intended 'total community and urban community was an illusion because there is no full community'. Peter Yorke (2000): 'in the original schedules for the Schools, no common rooms were allowed for... [because of the planned central Students Union]. [Later on] Schools were provided with communal areas only grudgingly, and on a small scale .... the larger Arts Schools were worst off... slum conditions around coffee machines ...' Further criticisms were that Lasdun conceived open landcapes and now there was a security problem. The Teaching Block: very deep, awkwardly shaped rooms... Nevertheless, the article acknowledges Lasdun's 'sculptural forms on a civic scale... masterfully controlled massing...' and provides, in the end, an introduction to what Feilden was doing with the Lasdun torso (see below). - The authors: Sheila Upjohn was the wife of a partner of Feilden & Mawson and A.F.Crawshaw was an associate of Robert Matthew Johnson-Marshal (architects of York University).

University most attractively, and at no extra cost, extended, as intended by Lasdun very early on, its landscaped grounds by creating a 'Broad' - the Norfolk term for lakes and inland waterways. [3]

Feilden's summary comment on his task was '... I take account of contexts. My values are flexible, but, although I fitted in with what Lasdun had built, I took my own line entirely on site development... From a town planning, a circulatory aspect, the basic plan for the campus was a mess'. Feilden was referring to his chief task to complete the University's centre. In response to the troubles, Frank Thistlethwaite remarked in 1971 that 'the University has been without a heart'. By late 1971 Feilden and his designers had provided it. Its layout provides essential links with his predecessor's, while in other respects it meant a departure from Lasdun's planning ideals. Lasdun, Feilden maintained, operates on a vast scale, uncompromising. Feilden, by contrast, prefers to operate with small units. In the university site controversy in 1960 Feilden had sided with those who wanted UEA sited inside Norwich. This went along with a crucial difference as regards the perceived behaviour of the user. Lasdun, according to Feilden, conceived of his users at UEA as 'walking briskly'; Feilden emphasised the stationary, the lingering, the sitting down.

As it happened, this change in outlook suited the task in hand, as there was only a relatively small space at the university's disposal for the communal buildings, namely the right-angled corner between the Arts Block and the walkway along the Library. Lasdun had always envisaged a series of large buildings to occupy this area, very closely placed together defining a square into which the pedestrian routes were fed with a street running to the North. In any case Lasdun's plans for this part of the university kept changing radically. Feilden dissolved Lasdun's vast building into a number of separate, independent structures, in the centre of which he retained a square of moderate size. He then extended the Square by a small shopping street. Feilden, however, did adhere closely, one might almost say faithfully, to Lasdun's walkway and vehicular access system, in the way the pedestrian access to the square neatly links into the given walkway levels. Finally, Feilden kept the buildings which surround his Square quite low so that Lasdun's mighty structures still look in; yet he put in his own high accent at the entrance to his Registry building.

3. The Broad: A lake was always intended but not thought affordable until Feilden discovered that there was gravel to be given away in return for the creation of the Broad. Staff from the School of Environmental Sciences helped with the planning. Landscape Architect: Rosamund Reich of Feilden & Mawson. In 1967 Lasdun had employed Brenda Colvin. The Geometrical Bridge over the River was given by and built by Atlas Aggregates. 'Landscaping' of entrances to Suffolk and Norfolk Terrace occurred during the seventies under Feilden by means of trees, shrubs in large block-work-surrounded beds as well as rocks. Lasdun's comment to one of the authors during the late 1980s: 'looks suburban ...'.

4. Building performance and quality: Feilden's special Report in 1974: Inflation, a two-month strike by builders in 1972, a shortage of raw materials, and a desire by the big building companies for bigger profit margins. Estimating and tendering became difficult. There was a shortage of skilled and unskilled labour, and firms competed for workers by paying ever higher wages and bonuses. The shortage of skilled supervisors, the practice of 'the lump' (a group of sub-contractors getting together, charging the main contractor a lump sum) led to inferior workmanship. The architect had to review the specification of materials downwards. Building costs rose faster than the UGC's expenditure limits. For example, the design and costing of Waveney Terrace had to be re-done twice because the architects, Norwich Partnership, were twice wrong-footed by the bank rate.

Robinson College, Cambridge, competition entry by Feilden & Mawson 1974.

Feilden took the term 'consultant' literally, and, in contrast to Lasdun, had his individual buildings designed by named members of his office and by other East Anglian firms. David Luckhurst took the lion's share. In terms of the extent of his contribution to UEA architecture he ranges third, after Lasdun and Mather. It would be a matter of a delicate debate as to what was Luckhurst's most important single contribution to the campus: his own vigorous designs for the Registry entrance and the Council House, or his Lasdun-like topping of the Physics Block. Somewhat outside Fielden's orbit was the Music Centre by a national architect with a very high reputation, Philip Dowson, which nestles in next to Lasdun's Squash Court, while also fitting in with Feilden's concrete blockwork. Its dominant roof matches that of Lasdun's Suffolk Walk Staff Housing, but it also takes part in the most recent architectural trend, the Neo-Vernacular.

What Feilden was most determined to do was to complete University Plain. It was a matter of honour for him to fulfil the task on time and on budget. Feilden, moreover, accomplished it in a steadily worsening economic climate, inflation, reductions in government finance, strikes, problems with the labour force, even uncertainties about the future of the University itself. By comparison, even Lasdun's later years appeared cosy. Finally, during 1973-5, just when UEA's last major structures were being completed, the government put the hatch down, i. e. it ordered an 80 % reduction of all new building starts.

An essential part of the new cheapness were the new kinds of student residences. Another factor was concrete blockwork, which was used for the great majority of the buildings under Feilden, whereas Lasdun used it only in his lesser structures, and, at the end of his phase, in the cost-cutting Lecture Theatre building. The interiors of Feilden's buildings are also finished in 'fair-faced' blockwork (even the study-bedrooms in Waveney Terrace). Feilden thus adhered to a general principle of Las-

Opposite: **'The Town Square of our community',**
**as Frank Thistlethwaite put it (detailed design**
**by Geoffrey Mitchell of Feilden & Mawson 1969-**
**71), uses the steep slope like a part-**
**amphitheatre which helps to create a feeling of**
**enclosure and also catches the warmth.**

dun's work, namely to use the same materials inside and out. Blockwork, of course, saves plastering painting, and thus, most importantly, maintenance. And yet even at this point not everything was matter of finance; there was also the issue of the quality of block laying. It so happened that the Musi Centre, arguably because of its slightly better budget, managed to 'snap up' the only two really capa ble blockwork layers, as a comparison of its walls with the uneven surfaces of most of Feilden's building will clearly demonstrate. [4, 5]

By 1974 we have come to another important point in the history of UEA. After some ten years th University had reached its initial target, 3000 students and £6.5m worth of buildings. The 'University ha come of age'... 'We are now an established University'. Most importantly, its buildings now appeare complete. But some of the high ideals of the 1960s had to be left behind in the process. Put mor directly, the quality of Lasdun's architecture had not been kept up. The key question is, of course, wa this due to a lack of design competence, or to lack of money? No firm answer can be given here; bu one needs to consider at this point two factors: Lasdun's style was going out of fashion; after all, Fos ter was soon to present something totally different at UEA. Secondly, we have to acknowledge that Feilde and his designers had decided to fit in with Lasdun's style. One only has to bear in mind the way in whic the Neo-Vernacular style adopted by the most notable Norwich architects from the mid-seventie onwards gained them far more recognition nationally and even internationally than the UEA building in their late Modernist style; Luckhurst had made the start with his Norwich housing group named Fr ars' Quay (planned from 1972). Dowson's Music Centre appeared nationally more successful precisel because it showed some of those Vernacular Revival elements.

'The emphasis of open days has changed', we read in 1975, 'since the early days of UEA, whe the main attraction was the singular UEA architecture. Now the entertainment is not the buildings them selves but what goes on inside them'. Feilden resigned in July 1977 to go to Rome and to take up wha was the most prestigious official international post in heritage preservation, the head of ICCROM. Ther was nothing left for him to do at UEA, and yet, this did not mean that architecture stopped on the cam pus altogether: the building of the Sainsbury Centre had just begun - and it occured at the opposite en from the Feilden complex.

5. Fairfaced internal blockwork was introduced by Lasdun upon Gordon Marshall's request in 1967. Arts II also shows blockwork inside. Building users, however, pressed for it to be painted. (Peter Yorke). Blockwork Report UEA 1974: 'Good workmanship with fair faced blockwork is extremely difficult to achieve. At present there are two workmen on site who I am given to believe are about the best we can expect and they appear to be unable to sat isfy us entirely with regard to the standard expected.' 'The Music Centre is distinguished by the excellence of the workmanship throughout.' Dowson's principle was to brief contractor in detail on what is expected from them and to have them produce samples that, onc accepted, remained on site and became the bench mark against which subsequent wor was tested. He also explained that good craftsmanship flows from the way a building i designed. He dismissed the argument that inflation and budgetary problems made goo workmanship difficult to obtain in the 1970s.

## BERNARD FEILDEN'S UEA

Feilden's 'heart' of the university consisted of a very complex brief of six major functions: governmental and administrative, banks and shops, cafés and canteens, student social facilities, an open meeting place and a large indoor Sports Centre. Feilden allocated a separate building for each of these purposes, designed by members of his firm Feilden & Mawson and by other East Anglian architects. Facing Lasdun's Arts Block are the Restaurant and Café ('Goldfishbowl'; 1969-71, by Geoffrey Mitchell of F&M) and the Chaplaincy (Simon Crosse of F&M., 1970-71) for ecumenical use, built after some controversy. Its costs were raised by a special appeal.

In addition there was an abortive plan for a large public venue across the access road, named Mackintosh Hall, in memory of UEA's first chancellor-designate. The great hall of the Sports Centre then took on some of its functions, while Lasdun's Lecture Theatre No.1 also doubles for concerts and other large events.

Right: Interior of University House Students Union in the early years.

Below right: The partly covered shopping street off the square might owe something to the spine walk at Lancaster (1970-2, by Johns, Slater & Haward of Ipswich, partner in charge: Birkin Haward ). The viability of the shopping centre as such is helped by an important planning decision, obtained by the University from the City in 1963, to the effect that shops were not to be allowed anywhere at the edges of the Campus.

Model of Feilden's UEA, early phase, c.1969-70;
Left: Lasdun's unfinished Library, right:
'University House', i.e. the Students' Union,
1970-3, by Johns, Slater & Haward; in the
centre: Dean of Student's Offices, Career
Centre, Bookshop, Restaurant and Chaplaincy.

## HONORIFIC ARCHITECTURE IN COST-CUTTING TIMES

On a campus in one of the full-blown Modernist styles one would perhaps not expect very prominent honorific buildings. Certainly this issue seems to have very little to do with the outstanding architecture of Lasdun at UEA. However, it must be remembered that Lasdun simply never got round to building any of the honorific, or perhaps more simply expressed, the 'social' parts of the university. It was under Feilden, in his second phase, that the buildings serving the university governmental and administrative functions were planned and built. Ironically, what one would expect traditionally to be the most opulent buildings were completed precisely at the time when the central government had declared a virtual stop to all university building. Lasdun, as was explained earlier, did care for expensive public or honorific commissions, but to adhere to a straight hierarchy of ornate front to utilitarian back would have appeared simplistic to him. If he had built his Senate House, or his University House as originally planned, the formal unity with the teaching block would have weighed more heavily than any honorific distinctiveness. In his Royal College of Physicians the honorific element is contained chiefly in an elaborate external and internal spaciousness. At UEA, monies for that kind of design would never have been available.

The Feilden & Mawson team, however, did introduce some measure of a hierarchy of decorum. There is a certain hierarchy from the opulence, or at least the severity, of the Council Chamber down to the look of utter sparsity of Waveney Terrace. One must not forget, however, that there is also a very significant sameness, namely the blockwork walls inside and out.

The staircase of the Registry is built up to provide a tower-like structure, in order to give 'an impression of entrance, and a sense of arrival to the University... a symbolic "gate"... floodlit at night.' The distinctive feature of the Council House is its impenetrability; apart from monumentality there is the desire to conduct meetings undisturbed. At the entrance to the Council Chamber we find a display of objects of craft and material value and complex meaning. The Design Report speaks of a 'balance between richness and austerity... individual designs... practical way[s] of introducing colour...'. There is a short stretch where block-work facing is given up in favour of knapped flint - a sign of East Anglia and Norfolk in particular. Bernard Feilden wanted to put a special stress on East Anglian design and building craftsmanship. The 'lay' Chairman of the Building Sub-Committee, Rowan Hare, masterminded the local donations. The Council Chamber is entered through a pair of enormously heavy doors made from 'Anglian sheet lead' which were given by Carter, the contractors. The outer ornamental doors in stainless steel by Neville Barber were donated by the architects. The seating in Council Chamber is by Brooke, the Lowestoft Shipbuilders. The University Mace (1963, Thistlethwaite: 'the University's formal instrument of authority') is by Gerald Benney.

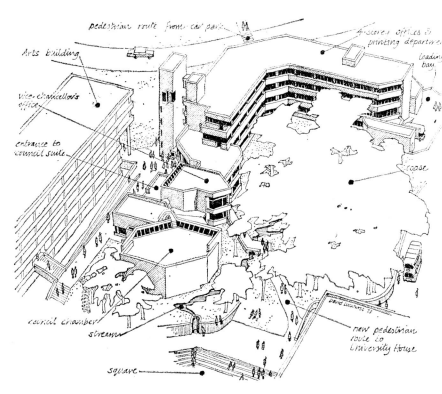

Above right: **The Registry and Council House (initially also called Senate House), 1972-4/5, by David Luckhurst.'**

Right: **The Vice Chancellor's Office, part of the Council House, with incumbent Dame Elizabeth Esteve-Coll (1995-7) The Georgian furniture was given by the Sainsbury Family.**

Top left: **The Registry, the main entrance to the Campus** (Lasdun's Arts Block II is on the right), drawing for Feilden & Mawson, 1972.
Top right: **The Council Chamber.**
Bottom left: **The Council House**
Bottom right: **Entrance to the Council Chamber**

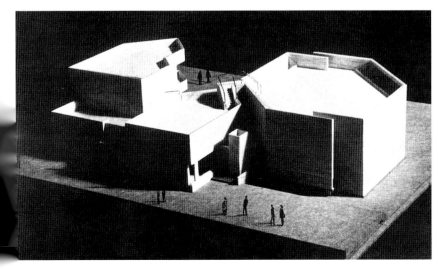

# ESCAPED TO
# SEE QUEEN

*There was no escaping a good view from one of the fire scapes at the University.*

'Escaped to see the Queen. There was no escaping a good view from the fire escapes', wrote the *Eastern Daily Press* on 25 May 1968.

Student Gowns designed by Cecil Beaton 1966.

Sports Centre (by Johns, Slater & Haward, 1970-71). showing a degree ceremony (1996). The earliest congregations of UEA were held in the medieval St Andrew's Hall; in 1973 they transferred to this building, '... the simplicity of one of our most purposeful buildings complemented the colour of the degree ceremony' (Frank Thistlethwaite).

## POMP AND CIRCUMSTANCES

There is much more to 'university design' than just plans and buildings. All large institutions develop a 'corporate image' and the image of a new university can be as colourful as that of any major ancient institution. Most New Universities went about purposefully to create such an image and the introduction of each new element provided some much desired publicity. The image of university pomp and circumstance, moreover, was one with which many members of the non-academic inhabitants in the region would be at least vaguely familiar. Frank Thistlethwaite was fully aware of this: 'Theatricality... my idea, everybody loved it'. Perhaps more effectively than any of the other New Universities (some of which objected to pomp on principle; e.g. Vice-Chancellor Carter of Lancaster: 'medieval nonsense' - but his students wanted it , too) UEA managed to combine old customs with Modernity in design, for instance in the case of the University Arms and the Mace. Thistlethwaite's greatest coup were the UEA gowns. Instead of going to the monopoly producer, Ede & Ravenscroft in Cambridge, UEA's VC went to see Cecil Beaton in London who 'was delighted' to provide a complete set of Modernist designs, ready for the first congregation in 1966, for students as well as for the chief UEA dignitaries. 'A peculiar mixture of high culture and haute couture' (Michael Beloff).

UEA procession, 1977, near the entrance to the Council House. (From the right) Lord Franks, the Chancellor, Frank Thistlethwaite, Sir Timothy Colman, Chairman of Council 1973-85

119

## UEA RESIDENCES MARK II.
## CRISIS AND THE WAY OUT.

Of all the problems that beset the University during the late 1960s, the creation of student residences was the most severe. It simply had to be solved if the University wanted to grow, and it had to grow, in order to secure its existence. It was imperative that it should reach its original target of 3000 within ten years of its foundation. Two further factors exacerbated the situation. Firstly, the New Universities, as we have seen, were created with an ethos of being a 'whole', with the ideal of the student living on campus. Moreover, the number of willing landladies in the medium-sized cathedral towns was limited. Secondly, monies for the construction had to come from the universities' own resources, and that meant the appeal funds. By the late 1960s these had mostly been used up. And yet, shortly later UEA virtually did achieve its aim to be two-thirds residential (64 %); next in the New Universities' league table was Kent with 55 %.

The Ziggurat type could no longer be afforded. Out went Lasdun's dream of row upon row of pyramids. But as early as 1964 UEA had acquired the lease of old airfield buildings four miles away, at Horsham St Faith's which with UGC money, it fitted out over 500 rooms. Students hated the 'Horsham Bus', and yet, as with so many makeshift solutions, these residences and associated communal facilities (especially the 'Horsham Bar') felt homely to many - something that was not lost on those advanced architectural critics of the late 1960s who so much doubted 'plannability' generally, for instance Tony Birks: 'There is no student objection to living in converted property'.

Then, by 1967, Lancaster had begun building its new type of residences which were financed by a loan, to be repaid through student rental income and some vacation letting. The cost of providing them was £700 plus per place. The 'Self-financing Student Hostel' was from now on the solution for most universities. Lasdun made an early proposal in 1967 (page 83). UEA then built its first new group at Horsham, the 'Z Block' (1968-9, Architects: Lambert Scott & Innes, Norwich; builder: John Laing, using a novel method, no-fines concrete) at a cost per student of £885. But the criticism from the professional architects' faction, in the

*Architectural Review*, was severe: '...Repetition of a very simple basic unit to suit the contractor's constructional method... a pity... the monotony of the long corridors and ranks of identical rooms... [no] experience of a memorable place... which students should have if they are to exercise judgment... in matters of building and environment'.

Another comparison well illustrates the scaling-down process. In the early 1960s we heard that student residences were generally dearer to build than public housing. With the Lancaster Residences standards had come down to 'Parker Morris', the 1960s benchmark of council housing standards in Britain. Horsham Z Block, it was suggested by the *AR*, was of an even lesser standard, more 'akin to those of the air-force barracks' around them'. On the other hand, the more anonymous block of rooms might also be seen as a new kind of student residence, as neutral background to student life, to the grown-up student who would reject the educational concept of the hall or the college.

Feilden then pleaded for more residences on the Plain. The University had to be swift because construction costs were rising rapidly. A group of 770 new rooms at a cost of c. £800 per place were begun in 1969 and completed in phases by 1972. (Norwich Partnership, i.e.Lambert Scott & Innes with Edward Skipper). The long block is of a similar central corridor plan, but not nearly as stark as the Z Block; yet here, too, sound insulation and the standard of finish is minimal. But there were new trends, too. Increasingly, students wanted to do their own cooking. The original facilities in Lasdun's Breakfast Rooms now seemed insufficient ('toaster used for baked beans', 'cauliflower cheese prepared in the kettle' - whether the blame was put on the architects is not known), thus the new kitchens were better equipped and Lasdun's kitchens soon had to be upgraded. Finally, the vast range of hostel blocks were carefully angled to avoid monotony and a grand name, Waveney Terrace was attached to it. 'There were always major debates about what to call things. After counties we chose East Anglian rivers. Yare and Wensum found less favour, let alone Tas, Tud or Nar. Waveney and Orwell sounded better' (Peter Yorke).

## RESIDENCES MARK III

In late 1973 a completely new type of residence was planned: Not a massive 'hostel' block with a long corridor, but 'terraced houses', i.e. self-contained units in which 5, 8, or 14 rooms were stacked up on two or three floors, with a separate entrance for each group on the ground. These units were grouped in complexes that looked like village houses, with steeply-pitched roofs and craggy gables - a vernacular revival style which formed part of a completely new trend in housing generally (certainly in public housing) - a style which at UEA had begun with the Music Centre. The cost was now £ 1000 plus per student which included some help from the UGC and the Wolfson Foundation (hence Wolfson Close). The term 'close', of course, is itself indicative of a changed attitude in domestic design. In the strong anti-modernist climate of those years it was not surprising that the groups were held to be the most popular of all UEA residences. Finally, UEA, like some other New Universities, acquired a residential foothold inside the parent city by leasing a recent Norwich council block 'cluster' of 1977, Mary Chapman Court - Hopper's Yard.

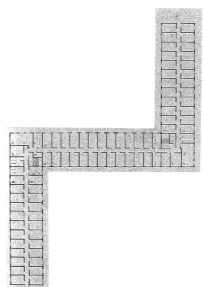

Left: Horsham Z Block Plan.

Opposite page
Top left: **View of Horsham Z Block amongst World War II Air Force Barracks.**

Top right: **View of Orwell Close / Wolfson Close (1973) 1979/80, by Anthony W. Falkner (Norwich), and (left) Waveney Terrace 1972, by Norwich Partnership.**

Below right: **A Waveney Terrace Study-Bedroom.**

Below left: **Wolfson Close / Orwell Close, plans 1973.**

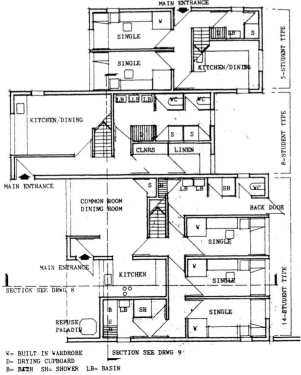

MAIN ENTRANCE

W

SINGLE

SINGLE

LB    S

KITCHEN/DINING

5-STUDENT TYPE

KITCHEN/DINING

LB LB LB    WC   WC

S   S

CLNRS    LINEN

8-STUDENT TYPE

MAIN ENTRANCE

COMMON ROOM
DINING ROOM

S    LB LB    SH    WC

BACK DOOR

W

SINGLE

MAIN ENTRANCE

KITCHEN

W

SINGLE

14-STUDENT TYPE

SECTION SEE DRWG 8

B   LB   SH

W

SINGLE

REFUSE
PALADIN

SECTION SEE DRWG 9

W= BUILT-IN WARDROBE
D= DRYING CUPBOARD
B= BATH   SH= SHOWER   LB= BASIN

## MUSIC CENTRE

1971-3, by Philip Dowson, who was given the RIBA Gold Medal as an outstanding representative of a private salaried architect (at Arup Associates). Not among his most major works, the Music Centre was nevertheless much noted at the time. £80 000 of its cost of £118 000 came as a Nuffield Grant. Project Architect was John Braithwaite, with the acoustics directed by Derek Sugden. Situated discreetly at the end of the Shopping Street, the Music Centre is reached via a small open-air amphitheatre. The main front of the building, with its pitched roofs, faces south-east and provides staff and students alike with beautiful views across a carefully preserved informal landscape. The landscape is brought inside, not only by the judicious placing of 'picture windows' underneath the deep eaves but also through the use of natural lighting overhead in the main corridor. The floor of that corridor follows the changing levels of the ground so that as one walks up and down one feels the ground beneath the carpeted surface. The windowless concert room is more than two storeys high and has a dark redwood roof of rafters, giving it a slightly chapel-like air.

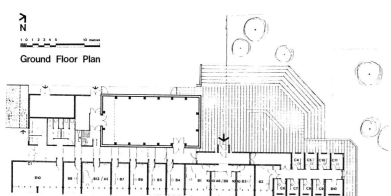

Ground Floor Plan

## NORWICH RESEARCH PARK

Perhaps somewhat unexpectedly, Norwich found itself among a group of pioneers of what was to be called a Science Park, and, very recently, a Research Park. As Michael Brawne reported in the *Architectural Review* in 1970: 'Universities have increasingly become places around which certain segments of industry and their related research institutes will locate:... MIT, on the fringes of Stanford, and beyond the University of East Anglia at Norwich...' The chief subjects here are agriculture, food and genetics, which relate to the dominant interests of the region and to the strong UEA School of Biology. An early decision was made at UEA in 1963 not to have them form part of the main complex. Most of the designs are due to Feilden and Mawson.

The Institute of Food Research (IFR, formerly the Food Research Institute) was designed by Feilden & Mawson (David Luckhurst) from 1964 and completed in 1968; it was meant by the architects 'to be complementary to [Lasdun's] University on the other side of the river'. It shows the firm at their most International Modern. One notes, however, in contrast to Lasdun's smooth 'international' grey concrete, that Feilden & Mawson's precast panels are of a brownish colour, with 'local aggregate exposed'. The large complex behind the IFR ('IFR II') was built 1988-90 (originally for the Ministry of Agriculture and Fisheries) by the Property Services Agency.

Near the top of the hill (top left) is the smaller building of the British Sugar Technical Centre, built in 1968 (Feilden & Mawson (John Sennett)) and 1989 (Feilden & Mawson).

Below: The John Innes Centre, formerly the John Innes Institute's first building went up in 1969-73 (by Alan Paine of Lowestoft). In 1988-90 Feilden & Mawson (David Luckhurst) added the Sainsbury Laboratory, the Cambridge Laboratory and the Library. The third phase consisted of the Lecture Theatre and the Nitrogen Fixation Laboratory (1994-5 by Building Design Partnership, with Anna Winstanley in charge). Luckhurst's lively roofscape can be explained, firstly, by the fact that labs need much technical equipment and this is best accommodated in the roof - as seen at UEA, across the river - and secondly, the architect had a theme of 'Dutch Barns' in mind.

# IV   THE SEVEN NEW ENGLISH UNIVERSTIES

## IN THE BEGINNING: EXPERIMENTS AND URGENCY

'Expiring dinosaur' (East Anglia), 'citadel of faded dreams' (Essex): critics and users of the 1970s have not been kind to all the efforts of the 1960s New Universities. In the context of our attempt to understand history by looking backwards, we may consider a very general frame of mind: whatever is the perceived 'speed' of history, of change today, at the beginning of the new Millennium, the power and speed of change were certainly potent tropes during the 1960s and 1970s. Critics perceived vast changes even when looking back for a mere ten years, from the mid-seventies to the mid-sixties. Coupled with the perception of change was often a rhetoric of disbelief and rejection. Discontinuity seemed to be the order of the day; though occasionally we also noted a way in which, at the height of a crisis, the Vice-Chancellor at Norwich (and similar voices could be cited for Essex) tried to calm the constant high pitch of expectations by declaring a state of 'normality'. And yet, the vehemence of all these condemnations can be seen as one side of the same coin: the sense of urgency, of speed and change was the essence of the creation of the New Universities in the first place. Within traditionally slow-moving academe this in itself was a novelty.

The development in Britain, or rather, in England, was a singular one. Virtually all countries vastly expanded higher education in those decades, but it was done chiefly by adding to existing complexes. All this happened in England, too. But no other country made such an issue of creating entirely new institutions. In the USA the foundation of a new university was nothing much out of the ordinary, but the number of big new initiatives of a major rank which also claimed a comprehensive new kind of institutionality was relatively small. In France a very large number of out-of-town sub-institutions was built but a greater number of new universities were only founded from the late 1960s. In West Germany there was a strong desire to create entirely new institutions, partly spurred by England, but by the end of the 1960s barely three had started teaching. It seems that it was only Canada which produced a New Un ersity movement akin to England's.

Much was made of the 'Robbins Report' of 1963. Internationally it was seen as a supreme example of English courageous and pragmatic procedure. Its chief message was simple: expand student
numbers. Subsequently the Seven were dubbed 'Robbins' Universities'. That, however, was to some
extent a misnomer. All the Seven had been founded before the Report was published, and most of them
before work on the Report had begun. Moreover, their very first programmes, during the late 1950s and
early 1960s, envisaged only relatively small numbers (for the 'University College at Brighton' just 800
students). When taking stock of their stunted growth at the end of the decade, roughly between1000
and 3000 students each, the numerical contribution of the Seven was quite small. Neither did they
contribute much, if at all, to the desired broadening of the social base of the student population. (Numbers of university students in Britain rose from 108 000 in 1960 to 228 000 in 1970, and to 299 000 in
1980; in 1950 the figure had been 85 000; proportionally within the age group the increase was from
7% in 1960 to 14 % in 1970.)

It was '1/3 numbers and 2/3' ideas' which was held to be the University Grant Committee's (UGC)
motto until the mid-sixties. Yet, 'numbers' did play a major part in the conceptions of the whole, as numbers mean size, and great size is too seductive a factor not to be taken up by most vice-chancellors and
architects. Lasdun's overpowering scheme was launched in the Spring of 1963, at a time when the new
Robbins' demands were already in the air; and Essex with its vast model for 10000, 15000 or more was
publicly launched at exactly the time of the publication of the Report. In that sense the New Universities were Robbins Universities after all. Or, to be more precise: the Seven English New Universities owe
their existence, initially, to a spirit of experiment which was prevalent from the 1950s into the early
1960s, within a continuing elitist frame of mind, and with Oxbridge as the supreme model. Paradoxically, but also logically, it was the desire to keep universities small which demanded new foundations
rather than just the expansion of existing institutions. But then it was the spirit of expansion at all costs
which came with Robbins and which the budding new universities willingly, and some even enthusias-
tically subscribed to. It was now the sense of urgency which was added to the spirit of experiment; a
combination that should justify the term heroism, at least in our retrospective view.

From our close analysis of the architecture and the institution we must turn to more general factors of architectural patronage from which the institutions rose in the first place. The terms patron and
client, however, need a lengthy definition. The actual patron was the state. The economically built New
Universities thus belong to the same category as state schools or hospitals; they may be called institutions of the new British Welfare State, as for the first time the state gave most of the money. State
dependency of all universities increased from 53% in 1946 to 83% in 1966; in actual figures, the rise of

that contribution was staggering, from £7m to £157m per annum. But once central government had decided to hand out the money, via the University Grants Committee, it was up to each individual university how to spend it. Thus we may rank the 'strongest' of the universities' founding Vice-Chancellors, notably Albert Sloman of Essex and Frank Thistlethwaite among the major enablers of architecture in this century. In the true English tradition, these patrons keenly trusted their own expertise in architecture. But the definition of the client does not stop here. In an equally traditional, or, perhaps rather in a nineteenth-century fashion, the architects themselves took on a role as briefmakers. A study of patronage traces the process of 'enabling', but it also deals with the convictions shared by all: the educationalists who formulated the principles, the vice-chancellors who administered the institutions and the architects who planned each campus - all of them subscribed to a set of ideas on how a new university should look and work. They saw it as their task to fuse the architectural and the academic concepts. The urgency of it all was linked with the conviction of novelty and each vice-chancellor and each architect prided himself on the uniqueness of their undertaking. Indeed, the Seven, ostensibly exactly the same kind of institution and built during the same years for roughly the same number of students, at the same cost, look amazingly different from each other (see pages 64-5).

The architectural patronage of the English New Universities - like most important chapters in the history of patronage - may thus be called a history of trust. To begin with, the state was confident that the cautiously dished-out capital grants went to the right agents. It had absolute trust in the central directing body, the UGC. Today we would probably call it a quango. In its day-to-day existence and its chief self-understanding it was a meeting point of senior dons from British universities at the offices in Belgrave Square, centred around Sir Keith Murray (later Lord Murray of Newhaven), its Chairman from 1953-63. De facto, the UGC was a branch of the Treasury; in 1964 it was incorporated into the Department of Education and Science. The other 'agent' was the local effort. In many respects, the New Universities carried on precisely where the last Redbricks, such as Exeter, had left off. But the national academic establishment had given them only slow, piecemeal recognition, and for decades they had depended on the validation of all degrees by a more senior university, usually London. Now there was a much quicker start. Complete new universities were to be had, so to speak; but the locals were now made to compete for the national money. The government, on its part, saved itself the trouble, first of all, of searching for locations, as well as a host of other local issues. By 1960 a great many towns were in the running. Their Promotion Committees had to come up with proof of: 1) profound and informed local enthusiasm. 2) already existing local institutions of an academic nature. 3) the likelihood of substantial financial donations and recurrent support from the local authorities. 4) a reservoir of rentable rooms for students and 5) a site. Thereafter local power retreated somewhat as the nationally orientated academic organization gathered pace. On the whole, though, the administrative structure of the New Universities was to follow the 'provincial', rather than the Oxbridge custom in maintaining strong 'councils', i.e. the governing body made up chiefly of local 'lay' members.

There was, however, a carefully devised rationale behind the UGC's choice of locations. Unlike the great majority of the earlier provincial foundations, the Seven were to be located not in the major centres and industrial conurbations, but in medium-sized, even smaller towns, preferably of the non-industrial, county-town type, and preferably in those with national historical associations. There was a sense in which the picturesqueness of a medium-sized town could be considered a national asset and a large cathedral, as at Norwich, Canterbury and York, is a building of national status in any case. That said, the UGC's stipulation to situate the campus outside the town, about one and a half to three miles, on a minimum of 200 acres (81 hectares) for 3000 students, meant that although the New Universities were associated with provincial towns, they were, in fact, not of the towns. Hence the preference for county, rather than city names. The reasons given were mainly practical ones, including that of pleasant locations to help with attracting 'good' academic staff *(The Observer)*; but there were also reasons of aesthetics, the parkland campus ideal, and, more importantly, of ideology. Most of the seven locations possessed a country house of some size on, or near the site. In nearly all cases these 'historic houses' provided the first seat of administration.

Thus we may call the whole foundation process a clever management of perceptions. The local elite of Brighton, or Norwich, proudly felt that without their effort there would not have been a university near their town (it would have gone somewhere else), while the state (or the government, of either colour) could be satisfied with the fulfilment of the 'national need'. And yet, the Seven could not be said to be 'local' universities – to the extent that this was seen to be the case of the Civics and Redbricks – nor were they ever 'state universities', in the sense of the new state foundations of New York, or California. Strictly speaking, there was only one major 'agent', the academic, or, to be precise, a self appointed core group of professors and vice-chancellors, exercising '*de facto* control of elitist institutions by like-minded members of the elite' (A.H.Halsey) and practising a 'hands-on, highly personal style of operation' (Michael Shattock). It was this group which made up the 'Academic Planning Board' (APB) for each new institution. Its main function was to devise an academic plan and to make sure that the independent institution would keep 'satisfactory academic standards'. All the Seven could receive full degree-granting power from the start. Finally, the Academic Planning Board had to find the Vice-Chancellor. Now, at last, the university was born, and it was 'born free' (Lord Fulton).

Some, however, plainly objected to expansion: 'University graduates are like poems or bottles of hock, and unlike cars or tins of salmon, in that you cannot decide to have more good ones', warned

Kingsley Amis of Peterhouse, Cambridge. But the university founders tried to counter the more-means-worse reproach with their stress on experiment. Murray's '1/3 numbers, 2/3 ideas' has already been quoted. A particular view of the history of English higher education arose: Splendid but arrogant Oxbridge and eager but dull Redbrick were constantly played off against each other. However, in many ways it was Oxbridge values that reigned supreme, values which were largely formulated in the nineteenth century by the likes of John Henry Newman and Matthew Arnold as well by looking across to the American 'liberal' ideal. The first foundation after WWII, Keele, closely followed the highly idealistic model - and remained suitably small and elitist for a long time. Its founder, Lord Lindsay, had come from Balliol College, Oxford, as had Sussex's Lord Fulton ('Balliol-by-the-Sea'), and in Norwich the philosopher and Dean of Students, Marcus Dick. Universities are ambiguous when it comes to 'Education' in the sense of pedagogy, but there was a strong sense of the educational power of the university as a 'community'.

'Redrawing the map of learning' was Asa Briggs' (of Sussex) most memorable phrase of those years. Under closer scrutiny, it was hard to assess what was actually 'innovative'. It hardly concerned the governmental structure of the institution. As regards subjects taught, there was the exclusion of the more vocational areas, such as medicine or heavy engineering, on the other hand, there were attempts to claim novel combinations. Each New University was expected to bring something "new". But the chief innovations lay in the organisation of the learning process. One could, of course, simply import the Oxbridge system and divide the university into colleges. Those who did not chose to do so, Sussex, East Anglia, Essex and Warwick nevertheless tried in a number of ways to ensure that undergraduates received a broader, and a more intense education than was held to be the case at Redbrick. The New University pioneers saw two enemies who were closely related, subject specialisation and departmental segregation. Departments or faculties, it was felt, were stifling institutions, here 'everyone was guarding his or her territory and change is virtually impossible' (Briggs). Now the 'School of Study', as Sussex and most of the others called their units, is a much larger administrative unit than a department and serves as an umbrella either of a geographical nature, such as European Studies, Anglo-American Studies, or it remained closer to the old division of faculties, as with most sciences.

In the normal sequence of events all this had to be in place before the architect was called in. In practice, the Seven, as patrons, were so keen on all matters of planning and design that most of them called in their architect at a very early stage. What characterises the Seven is that the architectural aspect is almost as important and as prestigious as the academic one. Put at its simplest, the Oxbridge men at the helm of the new universities wanted to rival Oxbridge architecture, too. It led to a way in which the architects not only planned the buildings, but prided themselves as the actual 'briefmakers'. A warning was seen in the way Keele had not appointed an eminent designer from the start and had thus shown a lack of direction and urgency overall. 'What is the Modern equivalent to King's College Chapel?' one of England's premier planner-architects, Sir William Holford, asked in 1964, who was at that time designing Kent. No direct answer has been recorded. But we do hear of the 'New University Movement... as exciting as the cathedral building movement of the early twelfth century'. There were, in fact, close parallels between the two groups: the top academics, centred around the University Grants Committee and the top London architectural practitioners, 'advanced' during the years after the War, 'established' by the late 1950s. Mainly through their most elevated mouthpiece, the *Architectural Review*, they obliged by pulling out all the stops of their rhetoric; from 1957/8 they put themselves into a state of alert, intending their contribution to university design '... to restore to the designer his synoptic vision and thus re-equipping him for his old role in the centre of civilization' (Lionel Brett).

Much of the most innovative university architecture of the 1960s, happened, of course, at Oxbridge. But we must return once more to the Welfare State and Robbins' ethos. The New Universities, by common consent, were built cheaply, even rock-bottom cheap. Comparisons with Oxbridge showed that the same task could be built at a 1/3 or even 1/5th of the cost. To cite just one example, in 1964 the eight-storey William Stone Building for Peterhouse, Cambridge provided rooms for 8 fellows and 24 under-graduates, all for a cool £100,000. At UEA, for the 'Ziggurats', that same sum paid for 100 student rooms plus one or two resident tutor's flats - and that in a building of an unprecedented architectural complexity. Of course, that does not take into account actual standards of space and finishing. The occasional chiding of the designers 'doing a Spence', to overrun just a little, is itself an indication of the prevailing cost-consciousness. Abroad, especially in Germany, there was great admiration, at least during the mid-sixties, for English low-cost building.

In the process of planning and building, the UGC proved its particular kind of 'double-face': towards the government and the tax payers it appeared trustworthy; towards the universities and their architects it could act flexibly. The university and its architect had to submit plans to the UGC at several stages of the process, which had created its own department of architectural advice and provided rules for a number of specific purposes, such as the minimum space of an office. There were also some standard cost limits. Each campus received a total of about £6m over about the same number of years and each institution topped this up with appeal funds to the tune of £500,000 (Kent) to £2.75 m (Warwick) and just under £1.4m at Norwich. All of which applied essentially until the mid-sixties when calculations became meaner and central control stricter.

Which, if any, were the architectural models for a new campus? The term itself had only just come over from America. The idea of a loose grouping in parkland was relatively recent, and could be seen in some of the newer Redbricks, such as Exeter and Reading. The older Civics and Redbricks showed a different tradition, one of densely grouped monumentalised buildings. The other major architectural type, considered thoroughly indigenous to England, was, of course, the college. Its derivative since the nineteenth century was the hall of residence which largely excluded the teaching functions. One of the essential elements in the planning tasks of the new universities of the 1960s was to make the campus as far as possible a residential one, without necessarily resorting to the expensive custom of the completely self-contained college. It was precisely the issue of combining the out-of-town complete campus with the residential unit that led to the astonishing experiments. The combination of campus and college finally led to a demand for the high degree of density; to avoid a '9-5' institution was the most cherished aim. By the mid-1960s the new, final ideal of a new university campus was an 'urban' ideal. At the same time this also meant the high point of the architects' input into university design (pages 64-5).

## NEW UNIVERSITY NUMBER TWO IN THE 'UNIVERSITY VILLAGE'

'A wonderful freshness in outlook, a splendid combination of curiosity and kindness, a self-possession without aggression, a natural egalitarianism without effort'. The journalist from *The Daily Telegraph* must have picked a good day to come to Norwich in November 1963. Pictures of the newly-opened 'University Village' are invariably peopled with eager and happy-looking students. The 'Village' which Norwich built with great rapidity in 1962/3 certainly put the young, small university on its feet. On the other hand, the Village also helped to delay the development of UEA's chief identity. It was not until late 1966 that Lasdun's distinctive university buildings came on stream.

Norwich could not quite compete with the instant academic and architectural success of Brighton, which took all the advantages of a first-comer anyway. York had been approved at the same time as Norwich, in April 1960, but took off much more rapidly; thus, in effect, UEA became Number Three of the Seven. All the New Universities were outshone for a time by No 4, Essex's massive campaign from late 1963. UEA's main academic concept, the 'School', largely followed Sussex; as regards its attitude to students it took a middle road between paternalistic York and 'free' Essex - although Essex must have taken more than a hint from Norwich for their new kind of student apartments.

This was, of course, a view from the outside. From inside, the picture is one of immense efforts extending over a decade before the completion of the first main buildings. Norwich had already launched a campaign for its own university just after WWI. A new attempt was made in 1947 with a submission to the UGC, but this failed because of the general climate of stringency. There was agreement that Nor-

# APPEAL FOR £1,500,000
## East Anglia University has £700,000 promised

**ANNOUNCEMENT IN NORWICH BY LORD MACKINTOSH**

**CONTRIBUTIONS PLEASE**

$L$ ORD MACKINTOSH (chairman of the University of East Anglia Promotion Committee) launching the appeal.

$M$ R TIMOTHY COLMAN (chairman of the Appeal Committee) speaking at the Press conference in the City Hall at the launching of the appeal. He asked for contributions "big or small."

Promotion Committee Session in the Council Chamber of Norwich City Hall, 1962. Much of the £1.4m collected was to be used for the Ziggurats. Left: Lord Mackintosh, chairman; Centre insert: Gordon Tilsley, Secretary. Behind the bench: from left: Lord Cranbrook, Sir Edmond Bacon, Richard Q.Gurney, Lord Mackintosh, Sir Timothy Colman, Frank Thistlethwaite.

wich had as strong a case as any. One complex factor emerged right from the beginning: there was not to be a university just of Norwich, but of the whole region; and 'region' meant East Anglia, stretching beyond Cambridge, as far as Huntingdon, and including the whole of Suffolk. Hence the university's name, which some were never quite happy with, as it led to confusion with Essex University because many would say that Colchester is part of East Anglia, too. Throughout the early years the authorities of Suffolk had to be assured that UEA was a 'truly regional university' and not just a university for the City of Norwich; it was even claimed that it was 'the only university of the region', because Cambridge was seen as 'a university of national rather than regional character'. This was of course rather at odds with the central, national task of all the New Universities and, indeed , students from the East Anglian region were rare during the first years. From time to time the academic authorities duly stressed that UEA also formed part of a nation-wide development; a dichotomy of local and national runs as a major theme through the early years.

At the beginning, local power seemed immense. There was no single dominant figure but a number of major players, though none of them with much experience of higher education. Lord Mackintosh was the leader of the team from late 1958 onwards. Son of a self-made toffee manufacturer from Halifax, he took over the Norwich chocolate factory. Primarily a businessman with little academic education, Mackintosh was nevertheless much involved in 'higher' economic activities as a member and leader of a number of public or semi-public national bodies, chiefly in National Savings and advertising. In matters of UEA Mackintosh was remembered for his expertise and enthusiasm, but also simply as a 'blunt, warm, shrewd, loveable Yorkshireman'. Lord Cranbrook, the chief Suffolk representative, came from a major landowning family, and had been educated at Eton and at the Royal Military Academy. There was also the Earl of Stradbrooke, Lord Lieutenant of Suffolk and Sir Edmund Bacon (Eton & Cambridge), who embarked on a distinguished military and commercial career and who, since 1949, had been Lord Lieutenant of Norfolk; Richard Q. Gurney of the family who co-founded Barclays Bank and one of whose former seats, Earlham Hall, was to form part of UEA; Timothy Colman, (later Sir Timothy) involved with Eastern Counties Newspapers, took on important roles, especially in matters of university finance: Colman was to lead the Appeals' Committee; Dr. F. Lincoln Ralphs was Norfolk's respected Education Officer and became the only local member of the Academic Planning Board. Norwich, the City, by contrast with the county, had been a Labour stronghold for decades but amongst its leaders the vociferous and cunning (Sir) Arthur South was one of UEA's most eager supporters. The unstinting secretary of the committees was Gordon Tilsley, the Norwich Town Clerk.

Over seventy local and regional notables belonged to the first Promotion Committee when it was properly set up in early 1959. The early culmination of efforts was the considered text of the Submission to the UGC. A continuous cordial relationship had to be cultivated with that body, its stipulations and hints had to be acted upon, one had to be constantly aware that there were many other applicants. A set piece of local organisation was the Appeal of 1962-3, this time the committee comprised over one hundred major names. Within a few months, more than £1m had been collected. Mackintosh had entered a bet with the Chancellor-designate of York, the Earl of Harewood, as to who would reach the higher figure by a certain date. Norwich lost this publicity stunt, by a paltry £5000, and Mackintosh had to send to his opponent a heifer from his farm at Thickthorn Hall. What is worth bearing in mind is that it was the Ziggurats that were soon to be built from that money.

Two major issues arose in which the local organisers clashed with the national powers. In late 1959 some Norwich architects came up with the idea that the University should be in the centre of the town. But the main Promotion Committee was not in favour, chiefly because the UGC totally rejected the idea; yet the ensuing public debate helped to delay the development of the University by several months. The other issue was one where Norwich won: So far, all the New Universities were to be labelled 'University College' - in the style of the Redbricks, in fact like all previous provincial university foundations. Mackintosh suggested to Murray that 'College' be dropped, and Murray followed his advice, not only for Norwich, but for all the New Universities. To quote a proud Tilsley: 'so what Keele and Sussex had accepted and York was willing to submit to, Lord Mackintosh successfully resisted.'

In other areas Norwich could not possibly expect to win. It was the national authority which established and secured academic standards. The Norwich promoters had, in fact, themselves been trying hard to engage academic advice from outside, and early on had created their own 'Academic Advisory Committee', with, for instance Sir Solly Zuckerman, the eminent scientist, Sir Roy Harrod, the Oxford economist, and Lady Lascelles of Somerville College, Oxford. One reason for their eagerness was that they all had holiday homes in Norfolk. When in the Summer of 1960 the UGC assembled the Norwich Academic Planning Board, Sir Keith Murray grudgingly agreed to take over just one member of this group, Solly Zuckerman.

These episodes can already be seen as part of an emerging pattern of clashes between the local founders and the national authorities. When the University finally set up its own government (in 1963/4) the local founders carried on playing a vital role, especially through the University's 'lay' body, the Council (taking over from the Promotion/Executive Committee), where they comprised two thirds of the membership, and in the Council's building and development sub-committees the chairperson was always a lay member. Essentially the role of the local elite changed from founding fathers to guarantors and auditors of university management or 'business'. In ceremonial events members of the Council always took first position. The first Chancellor-elect, Lord Mackintosh, was primarily a member of the local elite. After his premature death, however, in late 1964, Lord Franks of Headington, an Oxford man and a national political figure was chosen.

Academically, very little was happening before the arrival of Frank Thistlethwaite. UEA's Vice-Chancellor took up his post in October 1961. It was emphasised - just as well - that 'he has no connection with East Anglia'. He was a fellow of St John's College, Cambridge, a social historian and 'was known for his views about interdisciplinarity and his familiarity with American universities'; 'a scholar rather than an administrator'. From the start, Thistlethwaite entertained a sophisticated attitude towards Oxbridge, conscious of what he took from it and explicit in what he rejected. To many observers, Oxbridge elements could always be identified at 'St John's in the Fens'. The Vice Chancellor got on speedily with the main academic framework which was essentially in place by late 1963. The stress was, first of all, on the quality and the rank of the chief appointments. The other aim was quickly to assemble a comprehensive group of subjects. UEA started off with Arts and Sciences simultaneously. The concept of the togetherness within a large 'School' seemed to work well, particularly in Biology and later in Environmental Sciences. The University's image consolidated itself rapidly as a place which offered a wide choice, unusual combinations and novel preliminary courses. Frank Thistlethwaite introduced 'a highly articulated, Oxbridge-type system of student support with advisers, etc.' 'Face-to-Face teaching' was the ideal, tutorials, small seminar groups; teaching through lectures was greatly discouraged. Occasionally the Vice-Chancellors of York and Norwich went so far as to call their new institutions 'teaching universities'. UEA, furthermore, prided itself in having gone further in user-friendliness, especially by claiming a first with the introduction of continuous assessment, in fact, one of Thistlethwaite's Americanisms. At the same time the Vice Chancellor had to join in fully with the exhausting task of regional propagation, particularly fund-raising - '100 barnstorming speeches in three months' to schools and firms up and down the region. Corporate identity and external publicity had to be constantly developed.

Not everything, however, had to be new. As has already been mentioned, the UGC made sure that most of the New Universities were located in areas of historical and picturesque attractiveness, away from the populous industrial towns, so that they might more easily attract good staff. Especially in a remote area like Norfolk - more than in the metropolitan orbit of Essex and Sussex - the larger estates in the shires were seen, by some, to rank socially and culturally above the nearby towns. The reasons for placing the campuses in the country were thus practical, but also aesthetic and ideological. The rejection of the town centre site in Norwich to some extent followed the same thinking. In Norfolk this factor of moving into the country scene was probably at its strongest; not only did the administration lodge in the 'Hall' but the country cottage and farmhouse became the prefered residence for the staff, from the Vice-Chancellor downwards. At any rate, it all contributed to a good practical, as well as a socially convincing start for the institution.

By mid to late 1962, after its protracted beginnings, UEA felt a renewed sense of urgency. A momentous decision was to bring forward the admission of the first cohort from 1965 to 1963. Other New Universities had been using some very makeshift temporary accommodation; Thistlethwaite ('against the advice from my fellow Vice-Chancellors') decided to build a more permanent prefabricated colony of buildings which served every purpose except administration and student accomodation.

Thus New University Number Three, in effect, became New University Number Two. Only one year after Sussex and two years before York opened its campus, UEA was seen to begin properly with its first 112 students in purpose-built accomodation, 'a university in miniature', immediately loved by all locally, regionally and nationally, and widely publicised in the national press and in the professional building press - though not in the top-rank architectural journals. It was destined to 'foster an academic community like Oxford and Cambridge', according to the local press. But it also meant that architecturally UEA became identified at first with something that stood in complete contrast to the grandiose plans for the main site which Lasdun had first successfully shown in Spring 1963, and then to the vast concrete building site which slowly emerged from 1965. Many members of staff, after they were moved to the main buildings ('University Plain') during the late 1960s and early 1970s, kept sentimental reminiscences about the 'cosy Village' amongst Lasdun's strange concrete world.

The University of East Anglia in late 1963, situated between a 1950s council house estate and the open country. The University Village borders onto 'Earlham Lodge' and Earlham Church. Part of the farm buildings, left, were turned into an entertainment facility ('The Barn'). Earlham Park is on the right (cf p.142).

## THE UNIVERSITY VILLAGE

The site was given anonymously (in fact, by the Gurney family, formerly of Earlham Hall). £250,000 was obtained from the UGC (the eventual costs were £278 000 for buildings and £20 000 for equipment). The local firm of Feilden & Mawson was chosen and the site architect was David Luckhurst, who, as we saw, became UEA's chief designer in the early 1970s. Bernard Feilden was by then already a respected regional and national architect who was fulfilling a somewhat similar role at York, where he revamped Heslington Hall so that the main architects, RMJM, could get on with their design. The architects were 'easy to get on with' (Rowan Hare). The Village proved a challenge as regards speed, a very severe winter delayed the building. Very rapidly a small campus arose which won instant praise for its practicality as well as for its pleasant shapes, colours and landscaping. 'We were very happy with the Village - a lovely site and the temporary buildings were well-situated. I've never been so happy as an academic, lots of square footage!' (Prof. James Macfarlane). By 1964 further structures had been built so that the Village could now accommodate 1200 students and staff; it was envisaged that it would serve for at least ten years.

1962-3 also happened to be the time when nationally the interest in pre-fabricated 'system building' in timber or in non-conventional building materials was at its height. Medway were chiefly known to municipal authorities (Norwich included) for their two-storey prefabricated houses. The UEA Village's Medway System, predominantly of timber ('waterproof plywood and some Western Red Cedar') was considered a model of its kind. A major innovation was the installation of electric night storage heaters. What the look of the Village came closest to, was the prefabricated Hertfordshire type of school, famous genre of Welfare State 'social architecture', of a decade or so earlier - in some ways a fitting image for a new kind of 'teaching university'. The 'Village' gradually fell of out use in the 1980s and was demolished by 1990. Today's 'Village' of student residences was built by Team Management Services UK Ltd. ('Design and Build') in 1993-4.

Layout of the Village 1963.

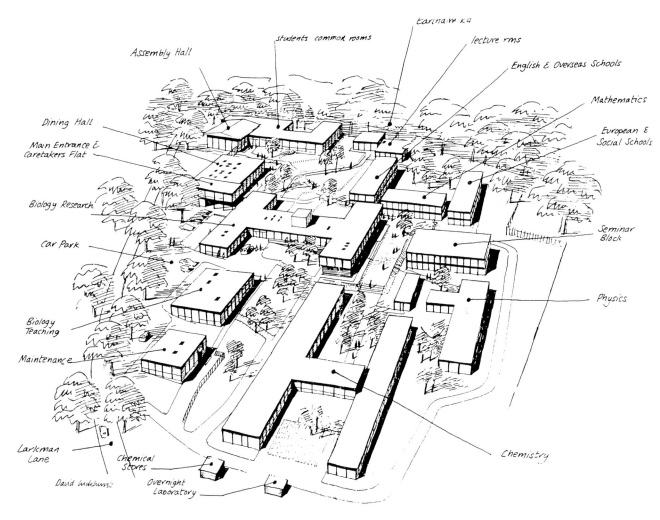

Assembly Hall
students common rooms
Earlham Rd
lecture rms
English & Overseas Schools
Mathematics
Dining Hall
European & Social Schools
Main Entrance & Caretakers Flat
Biology Research
Car Park
Seminar Block
Biology Teaching
Physics
Maintenance
Larkman Lane
David Luckhurst
Chemical Stores
Overnight Laboratory
Chemistry

University Village students, from *The Daily Telegraph*, 29 November 1963.

Below: **View of the Village towards the canteen.**

## FITTING INTO THE NORFOLK HERITAGE

The city of Norwich was surrounded by a number of hamlets. Their halls, their grounds, their cottages and small churches had not changed for centuries. One such old hamlet was Earlham. The Gurney family's home is architecturally not particularly distinguished but it contains precious memories of Elisabeth Fry, the early social reformer. The Hall and part of the adjacent land had earlier on been acquired by the City (for the Municipal Golf Course); the City now leased the Hall to the University and gave them the land of the golf course, to become the University Plain. Thus all of UEA's land had originally belonged to the Gurneys and Richard Q.Gurney was an important member of the Promotion Committee. Soon the university headquarters were installed in Earlham Hall amidst extremely pleasant and genteel surroundings. The low-density outer-suburban council-housing was kept at bay and the university planners subsequently made sure that they created a 'cordon sanitaire' (Lasdun).

During the same years several of the New Universities negotiated with the UGC with regard to building lavish houses for their vice chancellors; a major reason cited was the need for entertainment. Sums of £20,000 or more were allocated for the buildings. At Norwich the question also arose whether to build a modern residence for the VC close to the campus (as was to happen with Sloman's villa in Wivenhoe Park, and James's at York) but Thistlethwaite

decided he wanted to be more private (while still keeping up the entertaining) and soon moved into Wood Hall at Hethersett some miles away. When there was a plan for a residential development adjacent to Wood Hall (by a developer not connected with UEA), the UEA Council objected: '... contrary to the interests of the University'.

To own and lovingly restore a small manor house or Georgian farmhouse in the Norfolk countryside was a dream that came true for many a member of UEA staff. After all, untouched remoteness had been the chief intellectual perception of Norfolk for most of the century. During UEA's very early years Gordon Tilsley remembers receiving a letter from America, from an academic about to join: 'please find me a Georgian house near a river with a tennis court adjacent'. As Thistlethwaite saw it at the time: 'it seemed desirable at that stage of the University's career, for the Vice-Chancellor to be quartered in a house which was known to, and accepted by, the County, rather than in some town house in the centre of Norwich'. Among the university lay administrators Thistlethwaite much preferred the county to the city elite. There was then the intention eventually to use Earlham Hall as the UEA Faculty Club - it would have meant splendid isolation for the dons; but instead, Earlham Lodge, still somewhat genteel, served the function for a number of years while it formed part of the University Village.

Above: Hethersett (Norfolk), Wood Hall, 17th century, residence of the Vice Chancellor

Below: Aylsham (Norfolk) Abbot's Hall Farm, 17th century. Some time home of the professor of art history.

Earlham Hall 16th to 18th centuries. Home of the University Administration in the early years, now seat of the Law School.

Earlham Lodge, 17th century. UEA Senior Common Room in the early years.

## THE LOCATION DISPUTE

To provide a site for a new university was the task of the local authority. But the UGC firmly stipulated a comfortably large site of at least 200 acres which could normally only be found outside the town or on the edge of it. There was, nevertheless, much local discussion as to which site to chose. In Norwich, during 1959-60 a strong faction arose, mainly of architects, with the support of the local amenity society (Norwich Society) who pleaded for a university in the city centre, partly on a site along Ber Street and partly further out, on land that belonged to the Colman firm ('a university from a grain of mustard seed'). Its supporters even called in an outside report, by Bridgwater, Shepheard & Epstein (later of Lancaster University fame) and the *Architects' Journal* was also firmly on their side, admonishing the UGC to exercise 'greater social responsibility'. However, the UGC would hardly listen to this faction and the most influential members of the Promotion Committee, Mackintosh, Colman and Tilsley sided with the UGC. According to Timothy Colman some of these supporters envisaged 'dreaming spires and dons on bicycles'. A crucial judgment was also that a university on Ber Street would look 'dismal and unattractive and [would] provide unpleasant views of the railway sidings, the electricity power station and the new gas works'.

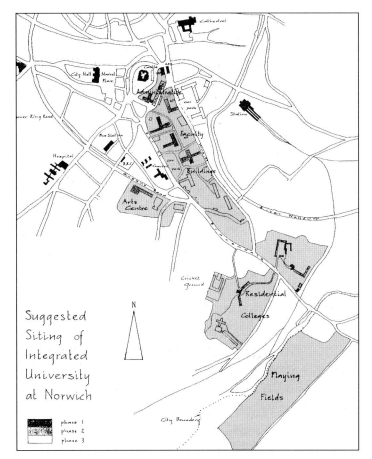

Above: Proposal for a university on inner city (Ber Street) and edge of city sites, by Bruce Henderson-Gray 1959.

Below: *Ordnance Survey* Map of Norwich and its Western fringes with UEA (Lasdun's university plain, Earlham Hall and north of it University Village) and the Research Park at Colney.

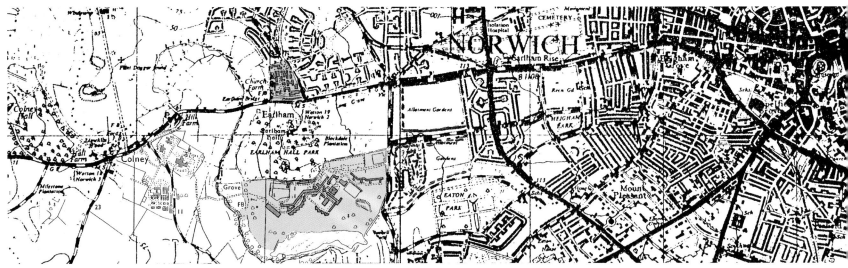

# THE QUESTION OF THE *GENIUS LOCI* OF BIG MODERNIST ARCHITECTURE, OR: PATRONAGE, NATIONAL, REGIONAL, LOCAL

V

'... every mile seemed to draw a thicker curtain than the last between you and the world, so that finally, when you are set down at the Hall, no sound whatever reaches your ear; the very light seems to filter through deep layers; and the air circulates slowly...'.

Thus Virginia Woolf approached Blo Norton Hall in 1906. Norfolk's crushing provinciality and remoteness was a standard English trope. Closer to our times, in the 1960s, Ian Nairn, one of the most sensitive observers of Britain's diverse topography provides us with much the same observations: 'Of all the places in England this is the most self-sufficient - you could tow Norfolk and its county town off into the middle of the North Sea and life would still go on much the same way.' An unusually frank report on UEA in *The Times* of 1963 (unsigned, of course) presented similar characteristics even for Norwich itself:

'...unusually high proportion of working-class members of the population. The town was several times described as "practically feudal" since many of the well-to-do lived in the country.... Norfolk people were "inclined to be clannish", though few were hostile to the idea of a university'.

This chapter attempts to get to those aspects of the meaning of UEA's architecture which are less directly linked to its academic institutionality. A discussion of the 'meaning' of architecture is, of course, also a discussion of the perceptions of its quality. But what would this have to do with 'provinciality'? When we harp on localism and remoteness, are we not concerned with the past, and with just the vernacular environment, or, as we would say today, with heritage, while most major buildings, at least since the nineteenth century, belong to the sphere of national and international patronage and are classified under nationwide styles of architecture; hence they cannot be evaluated in a purely local context.

Left: **Norwich from Mousehold Heath, by Arnesby Brown, 1934/5. Norwich Castle Museum**

Right: **Blo Norton Hall (Norfolk) , 16th and 17th centuries.**

As we shall see nearer the end, such a position can more confidently be argued today, but during the 1960s and 1970s matters were not so straightforward. As the story of this book moved backwards we noted an ever greater importance of the local 'scene'. A most complex situation prevailed, both as regards the structures of architectural patronage, and the perceived meaning of the building in its geographical context. The complexity of the situation could even lead to a frame of mind in which the very elements of great size and Modernist styles also appeared as signs of a *genius loci*.

In any case, we have to begin by stating generally that 'remoteness' always has its counterpart of a centralist, or simply, a metropolitan consciousness. What is unspokenly present in Virginia Woolf's rhapsody is that only a metropolitan person could 'appreciate' the local scene in the way she did, in its absolute, primeval remoteness, and that a local person could, almost by definition, not share any such perspective. Thus there appears an absolute polarisation between what one might call a local, vernacular existence and the metropolitan viewpoint. Again, the kinds of building discussed here could not possibly fall into the former category. Not only the designers, but also the patrons must be considered on a national level. We are concerned with a local and regional elite who enjoyed very considerable powers, financial, administrative and honorific. Most members of this elite were acutely aware of the polarity national/local and were conscious that they might be considered 'provincial' by the metropolitans. Their spheres of activity were, indeed, far from exclusively local, because, at least as individuals, most of them entertained commercial and social links outside the county, chiefly in the capital. And yet, in our context they were perceived in their limited spheres of activity within the region. It was here they wanted to be, and felt they could be, particularly active, and a new university was something they wanted for their region.

Furthermore we should note that our contrast metropolitan/provincial was linked to other kinds of cultural and artistic polarisations. The local/national patrons at Norwich can be perceived as of solid upper-middle or upper-class status, pragmatically-minded, with their chief interests in land and business, while sharing - at their own admission - only a mild amateur interest in metropolitan art and architecture (Lord Mackintosh chiefly collected Toby jugs, but also Norwich School landscape pictures). They 'clashed' with a volatile intellectual and artistic elite, intensely concerned with their avant-garde concepts and utterly convinced of some absolute values, social, artistic, or academic. The polarity explored here is thus a twofold one: an academic/intellectual/professional/avant-garde class versus a purely moneyed/landed one, combined with the polarity metropolitan / regional. It was almost axiomatic that the 'provincial' elite (and any subspecies of it) was lagging 'behind' the metropolitan elite in their cultural aspirations, and it was taken for granted that the latter would criticise the former. Ian Nairn had set out to praise historic Norwich; but he ended up severely criticising what Norwich was doing in the 1960s, what he saw as the insensitivity of the latest architectural insertions into the Norwich townscape; for instance the very large new buildings for the Norwich Union Insurance Company, or the 'crushing banality' of the newly-widened St Stephen's Street. He concluded his article by adding to the already quoted remark of the 'most self-sufficient city': 'It would be tragic if Norwich also became the most self-satisfied'.

The chief issue now is, of course, can there be a good quality 'local' kind of architecture for major buildings? From most chapters of this book we may gauge that the answer was: no. But precisely such a direct statement cannot be found. It would sound inequitable within a nineteenth and twentieth-century democracy. There was, in fact, no proper discourse of the issue national/local in architecture. The London architectural critical establishment had to be cautious with any overt criticism of their local or regional colleagues. The most strident sign is simply silence. A crucial factor which we noticed in the evaluation of Feilden & Mawson's work at UEA was that, however much praised locally, the high-brow metropolitan architectural journals did not illustrate it. But if the London establishment could not get at the 'bad' provincial architecture directly, they would still blame the provincial patrons - and this could include cases where the designer had actually come from London. 'The Norwich Union went to a big London firm and got a completely anonymous slab ...', Nairn continued his analysis; it was the regional patrons who could not be trusted and were openly chided.

Throughout our account of UEA we followed the issue of Norwich patrons vs. national patrons. There was a basic sense that major architectural decisions should not be left to the local founder-elite, and yet the local patrons kept on playing a major role. This was, first of all, a natural result, almost a built-in factor, in the way Sir Keith Murray and the UGC initiated the New Universities. The national patron wanted the first initiatives to come from the locality; the promoters had to strive, to compete for 'their' university and they did it out of local pride. In that sense the Seven New Universities were successors to the Civics and most Redbricks. On the other hand, the biggest of the Civics, like Leeds or Liverpool, had established themselves largely without central state support, they were embedded into very populous regions where they also fitted into an already established dignity of municipalism, based largely on new industrial wealth. The cathedral cities / county towns within their agricultural regions could match neither; their only assets were their old monuments and their picturesqueness, their vernacular charm. There were, moreover, considerable differences amongst the New Universities: Essex and Sussex, and to a lesser extent, Kent, were, from the start, considered very much part of the London orbit. York could demonstrate its own exceptionally strong historical and academic tradition; Warwick was, in the way of the Civics, more firmly linked to the culture of advanced industry and science of Coventry and its area. Lancaster, though distant, was at least placed on a major line of communication.

It appears that, among the Seven, it was the Norwich location where the 'provincial' element was strongest. Norfolk still felt wholly outside the 'London orbit'. Economically, Norfolk and Suffolk were per-

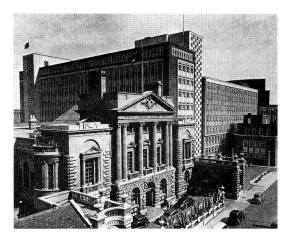

Norwich Union Building, Surrey Street, new buildings 1960-1 by T.P.Bennet & Sons.

ceived as a region which had remained what it had always been, agricultural, and no town had risen above the status of a 'county town', although it must be remembered that some centuries back the region's (and Norwich's) relative importance was very much greater. Academically, East Anglia had, in the past, served as a kind of hinterland, if not back yard, to Cambridge University. All the more decisive was the initiative of the local elite. A locational analysis of the principles of New University planning in 1974 restated the chief incentives for their establishment: the hopes for a boost of local cultural and leisure facilities and general economic growth, and a 'dominant factor of... prestige'. Subsequently, however, it was precisely the New Universities' desire for instant recognition as complete academic institutions (in contrast to the slow speed that the Civics and Redbricks had experienced) which meant the seizure of the initiative by the national academic - and architectural - establishment: 'the state effectively pre-empted further [local] discussion about the kind of university they [the local founders] would receive'. The early dispute over the sites in Norwich kept being cited, inner city versus out of town; the UGC would only consider the latter.

And yet, it was the Norwich Promotion/Executive Committee which decided, before the appointment of the Vice-Chancellor, to resist the pressure of the local architectural lobby and to press for the appointment of a national architect, even 'an international' one. The most prominent members of the local founders, such as Timothy Colman or Gordon Tilsley, had a reasonably clear idea that they wanted a 'Modern' building and they sensed that the supporters of the inner Norwich site were after an outdated image of cycling dons amongst church towers. It was suggested that sporting an architect of national importance would help with the local appeal. On the other hand, these patrons lacked detailed knowledge of the newest architectural trends, hence their letters to national agencies seeking advice. After that point, however, the choice, at UEA, of the avant-garde designer Lasdun, was that of the new Vice-Chancellor, Thistlethwaite, a member of the national academic elite, and the Cambridge elite in particular, where he was participating in a new wave of enthusiasm for advanced architecture. After that, UEA's polarities became more complex again. To the national client, the UGC, it was the whole of UEA, including the university committees, on which local lay members continued to serve, as well as the metropolitan architect, who appeared incompetent. But within the client group at UEA, the standard polarisation continued. The Vice-Chancellor was on the side of his artistic avant-garde designer, even though he and UEA fell foul of UGC guidelines, while many of the local elite remained sceptical of Lasdun, or were, as in the case of Norwich City Councillor, Arthur South, hostile to his designs - only to be bowled over by Lasdun's persuasiveness. On several occasions Lasdun voiced his dissatisfaction with some of his clients at UEA.

In the 1970s, at UEA, it appeared inconceivable that any further avant-garde building would be designed by a local architect. The Sainsbury Centre did not originate at all with a local patron. Neither Sir Robert

Sainsbury nor Norman Foster had anything whatsoever to do with Norwich or Norfolk (except for the fact that the Sainsburys' daughter, Annabel, had studied at UEA). The University authorities acted as mere executants; Feilden, then still UEA's consultant architect, was hardly even asked about the siting, let alone about the design. The polarisation was complete when it broke out openly in Peter Cook's praise of the Sainsbury Centre in 1979, and his denouncement of 'tweedy provincialism and technical mediocrity'- referring, no doubt, to Bernard Feilden and his colleagues. At the height of their influence, Foster's and especially Cook's metropolitan architectural movements combined the pride of utter avant-gardism and radicalism with traditional notions of the superiority of individual artistic genius, as well as metropolitan centrality and even a measure of contempt for the users' practical problems. At last the ridicule was not hidden any more: the local designers and the local patrons were openly accused of mediocrity and timidity. And it is only the locals who notice the leaks in the roof and worry about them.

It may thus appear that we have merely restated the hunches at the beginning: there is no real local or regional input worth mentioning, neither as regards patronage, nor in design; there is the eternally existing vernacular versus the rest, all of which comes automatically under the polarity national/metropolitan versus provincial. At this point we must turn to a kind of meaning which was always potentially there, a kind of universally-recognised generalised local element, which was usually formulated by the designers and the architectural critical establishment; thus it essentially formed part of the 'metropolitan' way of considering the 'country'. 'Genius loci' has been one of Britain's most cherished architectural and landscape values for nearly 300 years. Its very vagueness greatly helped its applicability. Principally, the term concerns the evaluation of the actual site of the building. It is the site which is quasi appropriated by the outside designer, it becomes part and parcel of the design. 'Genius loci' entails a declaration of a shared 'local' meaning of site and building. And yet, in the end, critics may infer from the site back again to the region. 'Genius loci' may refer to both an individualised site and a general notion of the unique characteristics of the 'genius of the place', even of the region, and thus it includes various manifestations of a regional art, such as photography or, in Norfolk in particular, the early nineteenth century Norwich School of Painting.

By the late 1950s the issue of the *genius loci* had came to the fore again, especially among Modernists. The *Architectural Review* and in particular one of its main editors, Nikolaus Pevsner, propagated the integration of International Modern with the specifics of the English landscaped garden. The culmination and conclusion of Pevsner's tract of 1956, *The Englishness of English Art*, is the conviction that Modernist architecture was predestined to fit in with many English traditions. What this largely amounted to was an intensified concern for form, space, as well as colours, while in practice it meant Modernist buildings sprinkled around a landscaped park, preferably an existing old one, which is precisely what happened at Sussex, and, in modified ways, at York and Essex.

The *genius loci* in Norfolk was, however, perceived to be a rather different one:

> 'Norfolk, with its huge skies and steely light has the most architectural landscape that I have come across in this country. It invites an unashamed building form: there is nowhere for a building to hide in the unshrinking panorama. This may explain why this particular area embraces the stumpy verticality of its medieval parish churches as enthusiastically as some of the most rigorously modern buildings to have been built in Great Britain.'

Thus Samantha Hardingham introduced, in 1995, her brief account of UEA's architecture. In Norfolk some designers and critics staked a very particular claim, namely that its landscape as a whole was eminently suited to Modernism. The idea was then given a further curious twist: Norfolk's landscape and especially 'its' sky gave rise to an unusual degree of monumentality. The 'Norfolk sky' had been a standard expression for some time, and a more detailed history of this cherished trope still needs to be undertaken. Wilhelmine Harrod begins her nostalgic *Shell Guide to Norfolk* by claiming that the county is not as flat as is commonly assumed, '... nevertheless, the most characteristic thing about Norfolk is its very wide sky'. The concept of the *genius loci* thus reached here a mythical, many would say, implausible dimension, indeed we may conclude that we have stepped beyond the *genius loci* concept altogether, the main ideal of which was, after all, for buildings to 'fit in', by being small, or even reticent, rather than imposing - while the Norfolk sky enthusiasts seem to go especially for the grand and imposing.

The plain fact is that Norfolk possesses a number of unusually massive and imposing buildings which, at least from a twentieth-century perspective, appear extraordinarily large if set in proportion to the population density of their surroundings. The story may be taken a long way back: Norwich Cathedral, Norwich Castle keep, the late Victorian Norwich Roman Catholic Cathedral. For the twentieth century we may begin with the large geometric forms of the Norwich public parks of 1920/30; in the 1930s the City fathers erected the most imposing of all English town halls of the interwar years in the heaviest proto-Modernist 'municipal' style. After WWII designers from outside continued the trend of severity, but now in full Modernist guise, the Smithsons in their School at Hunstanton and Reginald Uren in his Norfolk County Hall, a massive Corbusieran battleship on a slope on the edge of Norwich. Uren was chosen through consultation with the RIBA. He had been known for relatively advanced municipal work in the 1930s, such as Hornsey Town Hall. A vast building, County Hall houses more than 1000 officials. As with Norwich City Hall there was a long gestation period; the decision to build a relatively very expensive structure was generated from the shame of having had to put up with makeshift accommodation for a long time: 'rising from the Valley of the River Yare... a fitting setting for the seat of local government

Eaton Park, Norwich 1924-8 by A.Sandys-Winsch.

for England's fourth largest administrative authority' (quoted from the Opening booklet). All these buildings function primarily as symbols of authority and government. The much admired South Norfolk Council houses by Tayler & Green, on the other hand, excel not through bulk but through their long drawn-out horizontality. Invariably the photographs of the period emphasise the 'vast' south Norfolk sky above them. Again, it must be stressed that most of these buildings count among the very largest examples of their type in the whole of Britain.

UEA, likewise, is the most consistently massive-looking complex of the Seven. What is striking about UEA and its discourses is the way this massiveness is matched by the apparent strength of its *genius loci* claims. Lasdun and Foster would have vehemently rejected any reproach of disregarding the qualities of the site. To begin with, any architect's devotion to the site is a ploy to gain the goodwill of the clients, by praising something that it is initially theirs. One of the first statements addressed to the client emphasises the potential of the location. The University was also acutely aware at that time that so many Norwich people were regretting the loss of a popular golf-course. Lasdun, straightaway, spoke of the 'magnificent site'. Many visitors to his architecture have since echoed this and praised the views over the river or the Broad. And yet, in a cooler light, one has to admit that East Anglia's 'University Plain' had neither the large mature trees of Sussex, nor the dramatic contours of Essex, nor the special views of Kent's or Lancaster's elevated positions.

After the initial praise, the architect quasi appropriates the terrain for himself. Lasdun's as well as Foster's study of the site was intense. Theirs was a notion of pure landscape, undiluted especially by any kind of suburban development. Foster, with Sainsbury, made sure that their building was as far as possible removed from the busy east side of the university and turned a deaf ear to suggestions that the Gallery should play a link-role between the town and the campus. Lasdun had similarly demanded his already mentioned *'cordon sanitaire'* around his architecture and his landscape, so that it would not be encroached by any future ordinary suburban development - and we saw that even Mather, 25 years later, demanded the same. As at Essex, it was feared that the University site would eventually be surrounded by suburban housing developments. As far as future University extensions were concerned, Lasdun stipulated (quite in contrast to the early vast extendibility plans) that a 'Greater University' should look for new sites.' Lasdun even went so far as to claim that he had helped to preserve the area: 'West Norwich are indebted to Lasdun... for the conservation of the Upper Yare Valley'. For all its 'High-Tech' and factory-image kind of novelty, Foster's Sainsbury Centre, too, in its siting, continued the three-century tradition of landscape garden exclusivity.

'Lasdun studied the site for a year before they set any design on paper', 'we knew every inch of the ground'; we 'calibrated the section of the site ...' Lasdun concentrated buildings on as little land as

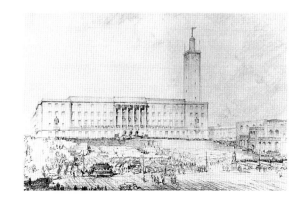

Top: **Norwich City Hall, competition design, by C.H.James & S.R.Pierce 1931.**

Above: **Norwich, Norfolk County Hall, by Slater & Uren, 1966.**

possible; in all ninety acres, of which buildings take only thirty acres - while at the same time his complex appears relatively spread-out. Lasdun, moreover, literally invented a special language to describe how he saw the landscape: 'landlocked harbour', 'swathes', 'the joy will be in the spaces between buildings, the grass swards,... the cascading terraces and elevated walkways ...' The 'aprons ...' leading up to the ziggurats and stretching around most buildings should be kept at all costs. Lasdun always elaborates greatly on the way in which his buildings respond to, and complement their environment, be it country or town. His approach is both uncompromising and subtle. Uncompromising in the sense that he wanted raw landscape, not pretty gardening and shrubbery (in the way in which, for instance, the University Village was 'prettily landscaped'); subtle in the sense of the precise formal response to the grounds. As has been amply illustrated, it is a general sense of 'horizontality', as well as the play on the slope of the land which direct the composition of the buildings and the walkways, while all views of the landscape are greatly enhanced by the way the observer is placed on the walkways above the ground. In the end, however, Lasdun's architecture always remained controversial, especially on the point of 'fitting in'; many critics simply denied it precisely that quality. Must the *'genius loci'* be considered just another element of rhetoric?

In any case, the definition of the 'Norfolk sky' and the discourse of the *genius loci*, as such, appeared to be brought in by outsiders, along with the whole package of points of view delivered by the metropolitan architects and their critical establishment. Virtually all the buildings mentioned here were designed by architects from outside the region. And yet, to a greater or lesser extent these buildings were, in the first instance, desired, or thought justifiable, by their local patrons. In the case of the City Hall and the County Hall, size aided the authority of a public building. In the end the question arises whether the massiveness, as well as the new and imported architectural style, is at least in part due to local patronage and a local desire for domination. The size and impact of Norwich City Hall had, indeed, much to do with the way Norwich felt that it had missed out on the Late Victorian wave of civic pride manifestations.

Perhaps a more subtle investigation of the *'genius loci'* and of the underlying motivations of local patronage will bring further understanding of UEA's shapes and their impact. The ever-shifting meanings of 'region' or 'province' might then turn from 'provinciality' to something more like 'autonomous province'. In the end the simple question is: do we have to see these large buildings as indigenous or alien? There seem to be two diametrically opposed perceptions of 'Norfolk': the remote, even hidden vernacular and the big open environment. The 'small' vernacular is definitely what is most cherished by those from outside; but the grand form under the grand sky was also brought in from outside. In our context it is the latter forms which are of primary interest. The key question here seems to be: how strong was the input of local patronage in the grand forms? In the Norwich site question the University's most important local promotors did not favour the urban site. Was, perhaps, the ultimate motivation behind the large Norfolk buildings the way the local patrons themselves felt the need to transcend their own perceived 'provinciality' and therefore called in designers from outside, in order to enhance the local impact of their own power?

The end of the 1960s brought some radical changes as regards patronage and the perception of the grand designs. In late 1968 it was largely the local elite who booted out Lasdun and installed 'their' architect, Bernard Feilden and his co-practitioners, all from East Anglia. It was alleged that there had been a lack of communication with the distant London designer, especially in matters of finance and in aspects of practical building quality. Feilden & Mawson's co-operation with the University was universally praised. By the end of the 1960s, polarities changed further. Lasdun's designs were now beginning to be considered slightly old-fashioned by a new metropolitan avant-garde who went in for flexible and unmonumental, even ephemeral kinds of structures. During the early 1970s, massive, undiluted concrete began to be disliked everywhere. This presented a curious overlap of laymens' or 'provincial' opinions (having their origins in the times before High Modernism), on the one hand, with those of some advanced criticism on the other. Furthermore, new trends arose in Late Modernist planning which stressed flexibility and the unplanned, even the spontaneous. A new notion of the 'urban' as a localised, even a grass-roots value led to new demands for greater town and gown initiatives. For a while, the 'parochial', the 'local community' point of view was 'in', nationally. As far as the main users of the university were concerned, the students, they divided into those who were contemptuous of 'provincial Norwich', and those who tried to take part in what the city had to offer.

How did Feilden's and Luckhurst's UEA buildings of these years reflect the changed patronage situation? The most important one, the Council House, contains a distinct token of the region, even of the vernacular: one of its internal walls is faced with Norfolk flints. The Council House specially documents and demonstrates the stronghold of the local elite, the local founders on the council. With its forbiddingly closed walls the building makes sure that it appears as a honorific structure, but one of a monumentalised, somewhat older style which Lasdun had left behind. Feilden's friendly 'Square' was more in line with the new thinking of openness and informality while the residences admirably solved the new problems of severe financial stringency, and even provided some practical improvements over Lasdun's Ziggurats. But everybody seemed to agree that the architectural value of these newest residences was low. There was a strong polarity, strong at least to those who claimed a special interest in architecture: Feilden and his local team, excellent at practicalities, speed and finance versus the architectural genius Lasdun, who, conversely, appeared less reliable in matters practical. Indeed it was the patrons' and the architect, Feilden's, intention to forego an overt architectural originality, in order to preserve the impact of Lasdun's design. On the whole, though, local pride and the disregard for what came from the metropolis were at their strongest in this period of UEA's architecture. 'Norwich got UEA because [it] genuinely wanted a university' a local architectural critic reaffirmed in 1972.

None of these problems occur if one turns back to an understanding of the *genius loci* in relation to the earlier mentioned love of the vernacular and the 'country', and the way almost all the Seven were initally installed in a county/country environment. When it came to the question of what kind of dwelling would make a suitable residence, Frank Thistlethwaite also opted, as we saw, for a small country house, for reasons of architectural as well as social prestige. As Vice-Chancellor he explicitly wanted to be associated with the county elite rather than with the city elite of Norwich. 'The country' and the county range above the county town. In the end, we may return wholeheartedly to Virginia Woolf's kind of appreciation of the country, of the minor country seats, manor houses or larger farmhouse-cottages. The many such residences of professors or even lecturers around UEA, some at a considerable distance from Norwich, seemed guarantors of private peace and bliss, especially when they were lovingly restored. It was the metropolitan-based Arts & Crafts movement of the 1900s which had helped to interpret the old rural buildings in that way. The frame of mind of the national, metropolitan, even international academic who chose such a 'house in the country', in the deepest provinces, was anything but provincial – as it was maintained at the beginning: in order to appreciate this atmosphere one had to come from outside. Private local bliss could well be seen to help with international professional success. In other words, the national/local contrast, or dialectic, worked perfectly.

Soon, this kind of love of the vernacular brought changes in the major architectural issues as well. All the problems of regionality and provinciality of an area like Norfolk soon appeared solved through the introduction of a new style: heritage. It was based precisely on the late nineteenth-century Arts & Crafts sensitivity for the domestic Vernacular but this was now also applied to all kinds of urban buildings, to housing estates everywhere, and soon even to shopping centres. It was a style that was felt to do away with the problem of the Modernist intrusion, of the new among the old, and of new buildings in an old landscape. Modernist styles were now considered unsuitable for all but the most urban surroundings. The immediate origins of this Anti-Modernism go back essentially to the polemics in The *Architectural Review* of the 1950s and the ensuing Townscape movement, and include Ian Nairn's writings. The new style was anti-square, anti-glass, anti-concrete. Feilden & Mawson adopted it for urban infills already at the time they were completing UEA, and it was this new local fitting-in style which earned them much more fame than UEA's Late Modernism. Other local designers, such as Michael Innes, joined in and Norwich soon acquired a national, and even an international reputation for its Neo-Vernacular. Lastly, universities like Warwick and East Anglia began to adopt this style for their student residences.

During the 1960s the issues of patronage gained momentum in the debates over the reform of local government. There was a profound criticism of the lack of professional planning competence of most local authorities, a sense that the complacency and self-importance of local elites was totally out of date. On the other hand, there was also a fear that the professionalisation and centralisation of planning expertise and decision-making might lead to a loss of the users' local involvement. All this came at a time when major socio-economic changes could be witnessed particularly in areas like Norfolk. Traditional indigenous employment diminished, suburbanisation and second homes proliferated; there is hardly any longer a 'deepest' country. In the strict sense of the term, there are no 'locals' any more, and it is much more difficult now to speak of a 'local elite' and of 'local' power. The introduction of a new 'heritage' style seems to take care of all problems of 'local' style. However, one has to be aware that, paradoxically, the heritage style is now a universal mode, or at least a nation-wide agreement, although it may, of course, be suitably varied to suit each region ('East Anglian Maltings'). 'Heritage', precisely, does not contain any argument about national versus local or provincial.

The chief concern in these reflections was to identify something in UEA's architecture that is 'local'. Arguably not much could be found, at least from our perspective today. Initial local effort apart, our institutions were shaped by designers and are used by academics, few of whom had or have much to do with the town or the region. UEA always claimed to be an institution of national, even of international significance. Much the same can be said about the other Seven: How much does Sussex's architecture really belong to Sussex? Or Kent's to Canterbury - while not even asking the question about Essex. As regards patronage, it is possible to argue that UEA's most important structures were built against the local group amongst the clients. Only Thistlethwaite and Sainsbury really mattered as 'patrons' in the narrower sense of that term, because only they were unequivocally on the side of their architects. International Modern was, after all, held to be precisely the least geographically specific style ever devised. Is the decisive factor in the final evaluation not the truism that architectural quality is indivisible, that it is, precisely, not locationally specific?

And yet, this is a simplistic point of view, supported, no doubt by a centralising modernist and even post-modernist art ideology. Any attempt to fully understand Modernism also has to take note of scepticism and adversity. If the process of patronage had showed a unity of understanding from the start then there would have been no place for Lasdun's rhetoric, there would be no need to cajole anybody into sympathy with the help of assuaging metaphors. Perhaps the simplest explanation of the capital versus province discourse, and its necessity, is that it formed part of a broader hierarchy of architectural design and architectural meaning. Modernist architecture, that is, classic international Modernism, like all traditional modes of architecture, imposed; and that in every sense of the word, including the impo-

Norwich, Multistorey Car Park near Railway Station, by Lambert, Scott & Innes 1998.

Holkham Hall Norfolk, by William Kent, 1734-65

sition of the metropolis onto the provincial sphere. In the end our simple question is: who appreciates UEA's early architecture and who does not? But a complex situation cannot result in a simple solution.

Today - and coming back to the beginning of this book - university architecture rarely wishes to 'impose'; rather it is expected to 'serve', and to serve pleasantly, rather than threateningly or 'heroically'. There does not seem an issue of local vs. national patronage anymore; even the most ingenious interpretation would not succeed in teasing such a meaning out of the recent structures. The term provincial is not heard in any recent context. Actual locality matters less and less. But where do we stand now as regards the *genius loci* meaning, or other ways of appreciation, of Lasdun's and Fosters' structures? Clearly, not by any stretch of the imagination could they join Virginia Woolf's cherished Norfolk vernacular. But they might eventually enter the company of some earlier massive regionalist Norfolk structures, imposed on the local scene by local patrons, but employing metropolitan designers. That would keep them in good company, though the process of appreciation may still take some time: as late as 1957 Lady Wilhelmine Harrod concluded about Holkham Hall: '... William Kent's masterpiece, never much admired by the neighbours'.

*Eastern Daily Press* 10-3-1962:
**'Up to 8 years for Concept to Become Reality.**
**UNIVERSITY PLAN UNDER WAY.**
Eminent Architect Appointed for East Anglia Project from our London Staff.

A Master plan for the new University of East Anglia should be ready within a year. Altogether, it will probably take seven or eight years for the whole concept to become reality. This time scale was suggested by Mr Denys Lasdun, the distinguished architect whose firm, Denys Lasdun & Partners, has been appointed to design the University. He and his team will be spending long periods in Norwich, and expect to start work there very soon. "There will be no question of trying to create a university for Norwich at long distance ," he said. At first he will work with four or five assistants; later they will build to a dozen. Mr Lasdun, who is 47, is a Fellow of the Royal Institute of British Architects. He has given London some of its most admired buildings. His first notable post-war achievement was the Hallfield housing estate and school at Paddington. "The important thing is not the building but what goes on inside it. But I hope what you say of Hallfield may prove true in Norwich. We shall have far more freedom than if we were next door to the Cathedral, for instance" he said. "There is little of distinction there except Earlham Hall." His freedom is increased by the scarcity of precedents for new universities. This does not mean that Mr Lasdun has a ready-made vision of what he hopes the University will look like. He distrusts that kind of approach. A university worthy of Norwich will not be done by its architect alone," he said. "The Vice-Chancellor, the board, the academic board, and others will all be part and parcel of the design team. There will be the city and its future to consider, and its chief architect and planning advisers will come into the picture. Ultimately we, as architects, have to make it into a built form, but it will be the end of a long journey of research". Mr Lasdun admits to being a person who thinks of his architecture as regional. He would not conceive the same building for the harsh North as for the milder South. What he builds in East Anglia will presumably show a regional influence but what kind of influence he cannot say until he has made his study.

Of all his works, Mr Lasdun finds his work in England most satisfying. While denying vigorously that he belongs to any particular school, he does not disguise his admiration of English architects. When asked whether such highly praised innovators as Frank Lloyd Wright have helped to shape his style, Mr Lasdun asserted his preference for the pupil of Wren. "Hawksmoor was a far greater architect than Frank Lloyd Wright - and you can quote me" he said. "The greater modern movements fired my youth but now I am past my youth and I think for myself". "But architecturally I am now entirely independent of my teachers. I have been for five years. I am very much concerned with rather special values, solely, or mostly, applying to England." He and his team are already studying the special values applying in East Anglia. "We are getting mentally prepared now and are reading a lot." as he put it. Those who have seen his buildings and the models of buildings yet to come will agree that Norwich can expect its new University to be thoughtful, vigorous and devoid of clichés.'

**ABBREVIATIONS**

AA (1967)   M.Brawne (ed.), *University Planning and Design. A Symposium*, Architectural Association [London] *Paper* Number 3, 1967 [mainly papers of a Conference at Sussex University 1964].

AD          *Architectural Design*
AJ          *Architects Journal*
AR          *Architectural Review*
ABN         *Architect and Building News*
Birks       T.Birks, *Building the New Universities*, Newton Abbot 1972
B           *The Builder*
Curtis (1994) W.Curtis, *Denys Lasdun*, 1994
EDP         *Eastern Daily Press*
EEN         *Eastern Evening News*
Est         UEA Estate Archives
F&M         Feilden & Mawson
FT          Frank Thistlethwaite
Int.        Interview
PRO         Public Record Office (London)
RIBA        Royal Institute of British Architects
SCVA        Sainsbury Centre for the Visual Arts
T           *The Times*
TES         *Times Educational Supplement*
THES        *Times Higher Education Supplement*
VC          Vice-Chancellor
VC Rep.     *Vice-Chancellor's Report*
UGC         University Grants Committee
UQ          *University Quarterly*

N.B. There is no room here to cite systematically the vast number of references to UEA's buildings in the national architecture and building journals, many of which contain a much larger amount of detail than is possible to present here. Consult the RIBA indexes. Nor can we give ample coverage of newspaper references (see UEA Press Cuttings Collection Library Archives).

**PAGES 10-15 MILLER MATHER** 'There is ample cycle parking ...': see page 74. 'New University movement ...': *AA* (1967) 7. Rick Mather Architects, *Development Plan for the University of East Anglia June 1989* (p. 44 for quote); *Illustrative Supplementary Material*, October 1990. 'Teaching Wall... stand alone ...': *Building Design* No 1011, 9-11-1990. Elizabeth Fry's competition: the judges: Derek Burke, John Tarrant (Pro-Vice Chancellor) (info Peter Yorke). On Miller: *Architecture of Discretion*, 9H Gallery (eds.,

London), Whitechapel Art Gallery Colquhoun + Miller, 1985. E.Fry and Queen's Buildings: *AJ* 15-6-1995 31-8; *Casabella* 6-1995 52-65, cf. S.Roaf, *Energy Efficient Buildings. A Design Guide*, Oxford 1992. 'The approach must be ...': Andy Ford of Fulcrum Engineering Partnership, *Building Services* 4-1995 19-23. Mather's Residences: *AJ* 28-4-1993 43-55. 'Incredibly high standard ...': *RIBA Journal* 2-1994 26; *Building Services Journal* 4-1998 37-42. RIBA / Architecture Centre (eds.), *Building for Higher Education*, [1996]; cf. Royal Fine Arts Commission (Forew. by Lord St.John of Fawsley), *Design Quality in Higher Education Buildings*, publ. T.Telford London 1996. 'Building Procurement': A.P.Fawcett *AJ* 15-3-1995 36.

**PAGES 22-23** 'Development... master': G.Darley, 'Visions, Prospects and Compromises', *Higher Education Quarterly*, Autumn 1991 362. H.Pearman (Foreword), *R.Mather*, 1992; K.Powell, 'The quiet Londoner', *AJ* 15-7-1999 25-6. *Architectural Record* 11-1985 97-103; *AJ* 5-3-1986 37-73. 'Expect less ...': *Building Design* 3-2-1984 10-1. 'Backland spaces ...': *Financial Times* 13-1-1986. 'Temple of the Winds': G.Darley, *op. cit..* 'Determined to do a ...'; 'something that has both ...': *Building Design* 3-2-1984 10-1. 'Frisson ...': *RIBA Journal* 2-1986 7.

**PAGES 28-35 FOSTER** *Catalogue of Sainsbury Collection, Exhibtion... April 1978* (publ. by UEA / A.Zwemmer Ltd.); I. Lambot (ed.), *Foster Associates Buildings and Projects 1971-78*, (Vol. 2) 1990; S.Williams, *Hong Kong Bank 1989*; R.Banham (Introd.), *Foster Associates*, RIBA Publications 1979. 'Building rooted ...': *Architecture as Building. Sir Norman Foster and Partners ...*, (publ. Sir Norman Foster and Partners Publications 1993) 25. 'Toughest clients... friends ...': Address by Foster at SCVA 28-6-1996. Sainsbury: 'proud ...' *Foster Associates Six Architectural Projects 1975-1985*, Cat. Exh. SCVA 1985.'Their own involvement...': int. Foster. 'Who frankly admits ...': *Sunday Times* 2-4-1978. '... Met rarely ...': *FT*, Confidential Memorandum 3-7-1996.Siting: Minutes of SCVA Building Committee 8-10-1978; *AD* 3/4-1979 92. 'Excited by Lasdun...': *EDP* 6-4-1978. 'Own building': *Mandate* 18-3-21969. 'Liberal education ...'; 'scholarship ..:'; 'I have never regarded ...': UEA Newsletter 21-4-1978. '... Ashmole at Oxford ...': *EDP* 6-4-1978; cf. *EEN* 26-

11-1973. 'We want to give some ...': R. and *L.Sainsbury Collection*, Exhibtion, 1978 Cat..'A new university...': ibid. 'There was an obvious distaste ...': ibid. 'Social' qualities ...': *AD* 3/4-1979 92. 'Not just a stuffy ...': *EDP* 6-4-1978. Stipulation... children: *AD* 3/4 -1978 92-3. Sainsbury on Brief: SCVA Building Committee 8-10-1974. The idea excited ...: int. Foster. A mid-1975 account: W.Foster, 'Sainsbury Centre ....' *AD* 8-1975 842-6. 'Costs confidential': *Foster, Architecture as Building. Sir Norman Foster and Partners...* (publ. Sir Norman Foster and Partners Publications 1993) 25. 'Original estimate £1.9m ...': *Contract Journal* 23-6-1977 20-1. The total cost ...: *Sunday Times* 2-4-1978; cf. University Newsletter 21-4 1978. On SCVA: *AD* 2-1979 (2ff.): Rogers: p. 30. Maxwell: p. 36. McKean: p. 31. Peckham: 2ff. Report from John Mitchell and Alex Potts for School Board 2-12-1977. A.Potts and E.Fernie, *Survey of Faculty, Staff and Students in the Art History Sector of the SCVA* 30-10-1978. A.Martindale letter Sainsbury Centre Board, 1-2-1979. Joint Shop Stewards Committte ASTM, CSEU, NALGO, NUPE and the Student's Union, undated [c.1978]. 'The combination ...': *AD* 8-1975 482. Contradictions Foster: *AD* 11-1972 no p. no. [inside cover]. 'Absence of air conditioning ...': *EDP* 6-4-1978. Pawley: *AJ* 4-7-1984 39-44. Ventilators colossal: int. Peter Lasko 1997. Foster 'always ready ...': Architecture as Buildings. Foster Associates Six Architectural Projects 1975-85 Cat. SCVA 1985. P.Cook 'tweedy provincialism ...': *AR* 12-1978 355-6. Feilden on Foster: Council Minutes 20-3-1987. 'Foster sheds its skin': *AJ* 7-10-1987 9, 14-10-1987 11; *Building* 16-10-1987 10; on original panels: *Design* 6-1978, 7-1978. 'Extraneous, but necessary ...': S.Williams, *Hong Kong Bank*, 1989.

**PAGE 38** N.Foster in *Contract Journal* 23-6-1977 20-1; *British Plastics and Rubber* 2-1979 32-3; S.Wiliams, Hong Kong Bank, 1989 67. 'In search for perfect skin ...': D.Treiber, *Norman Foster*, 1995 47.

**PAGE 46** 'Finite object ...': Foster, *op. cit.* 1993.
**PAGES 48-139 LASDUN ETC.**

F. Thistlethwaite, *Origins. A Personal Reminiscence of UEA's Foundation*, publ. by F.T. Cambridge 2000. Local architects: J. Fletcher-Watson 12-3-1959; E.R.Crane 10-11-1961. National/international: Tilsley 10-11-1961.

T.Colman: 'go national ...': Colman to FT 30-10-1961. G.Oddie in Tilsley note 21-4-1961. On Cambridge: P.Booth & N.Taylor, *Cambridge New Architecture*, 1970. Sir J.Cockcroft 25-6-1961. Tilsley to Martin 28-6-1961, 1-7-1961. Memo of Martin meeting on 8-7-1961: 10-7-1961. Martin to Tilsley: 27-7-1961; cf. memo Martin, Mackintosh, FT 3-10-1961. Holford to Mackintosh 29-11-1961. T Colman to FT 30-10-1961. Lasdun to FT 3-11-1961; 17-11-1961; 5-12-1961; Lasdun to Tilsley 27-12-1961; FT to Lasdun 3-12-1961; Mackintosh to Lasdun 1-12-1961; 4-1-1962; Tilsey to Lasdun 13-1-1962. (All in Est FN / 213.) Cf. Univ. College of East Anglia Promotions Committee meeting with UGC Report 27-5-1960 ('Brown Book' in Registry). Martin: 'I must have ...': Int. Martin 1996. Tilsley: 'We were shown ...': Int. Tilsley 1996. FT: 'aim of a high degree ...': 'Topics for Discussion', Special Council Meeting 2-12-1968 Council Minutes. On Lasdun: Curtis (1994); *D.Lasdun. A Language and a Theme*, Cat. RIBA 1976. Fees: Letters early 1962 (Est FN / 213); Lasdun 23 -9-1963 (Est FN / 213); N.D.Wolfenden / UGC to G.Marshall 30-1-1964 (Registry Archives). Lasdun's 'Draft I' in the Press: *TES* 26-4-1963; 21-6-1963; T 26-4-1963; *Guardian* 26-4-1963; *Observer* 21-4-1963; B 3-5-1963 875-7; *ABN* 1-5-1963; *AJ* 8-5-1963 976-7; *Surveyor* 4-5-1963; *EEN* 25-4-1963; *EDP* 26-4-1963; *AD* 6-1963 252. Lasdun's expectations: Report Committee of the Appointment of the Architect 5-11-1963: 'Lasdun, the Basic Facts of Performance' and Report 15-11-1963 (Lasdun mid-1960s file Est Archives). 'A Master Plan to be ready within a year.' Executive Comm. Extraordinary Meeting Statement by Univ. Architect 29-7-1966 (Est FN / 213). Centre Model in Est c. early 1963, ill. in *EDP* 26-4-1963. Cockshy Schedules: letter FT to Lasdun 23-8-1962 (Est FN / 213). The VC after arrival in 1961: *East Anglian Daily Times* 26-8-1961; Birks 1972, cf. Curtis on Lasdun's National Theatre: 'there was no clear initial brief.': Curtis (1994) 116-9. Lasdun, Memorandum D.Lasdun & Partners 5-3-1962 (Est FN / 213). 'Development Plan': PRO UGC 7 440. FT in on page 4: 'we have a Development Plan...'; on page 5 Lasdun: 'there is no Development Plan.' Executive Comm. Extraordinary Meeting Minutes 29-7-1966 (Est FN / 213). 'Effective pattern of committees ...': Tilsley to Mackintosh

12-1-1962 (Est FN / 213).

Planner-Architect problem: Murray internal note 19-1-1962 PRO UGC 7 213; cf. Report Comm. Appointment of the Architect to Executive Comm. 15-11-1963. Spring 1963: All PRO UGC 7 440: 'Confidential East Anglia': 20-2-1963; memo 1-3-1963; Murray to FT 13-3-1963, dto. 1-5-1963; memo 6-5-1963; Note of meeting UGC with Lasdun ('twenty drafts') and FT 10-5-1963; note 27-6-1963. Late 1963: Executive Comm. Extraordinary Meeting Minutes 30-9-1963. Tape-recording of Lasdun's address (in Est), also Minutes ('Brown Book' Registry). South's comments: Minutes 30-9-1963, also int. South 1997. Lasdun: 'shuffling around ...': Minutes 30-9-1963, 'Cathedral colour ...': int. J. Macfarlane 1997.

'Terms of apointment ...': Executive Meeting 7-10-1963. Lasdun's 'conditions': Meeting of officers with Lasdun 31-10-1963. 'Lasdun: Basic Facts of Performance': Meeting Comm. Meeting Appointment of Architect 5-11-1963 (in Lasdun mid-sixties File in Est). J.F.Cory Dixon, *Building for and by Degrees. A Client's Experiences on Building for Universities*, publ. University of Surrey [n.d. c. 1978] (RIBA Library copy). 'Almost in an 19th century way': int. FT 1996. 'A meeting of minds': FT on UEA, in: M.G.Ross, *New Universities in the Modern World*, 1966, p. 65. 'Your plan accurately ....': Minutes Site Development Comm. 5-11-1963.

'The Library ...': int. J. Macfarlane 1995. 'Lasdun: Basic Facts... Performance': Lasdun: Meeting 5-11-1963 (in Lasdun mid-sixties file in Est). For the Ziggurats see page 84. 1964 opinion of UGC: PRO UGC 7 441 memo 16-10-1964. Lasdun prefabrication: Site Development Committee Minutes 24-2-1964.

FT: Lasdun's scheme built together: PRO UGC 7 441 5-4-1964. UEA to be given by UGC £1.250.000 for period January 1965 to 31 March 1966 (PRO, UGC 7 441, 25-5-1964) and £1m for period April 1966 to March 1967: PRO UGC 7 441 14-10-1964, 2-12-1964.

Building progress in University Plain Development Plan, statement by the University 19-8-1966; *VC Rep.* 67-8. See in University House, Sketch Design, March 1967; *VC Rep* 1967-8; TES 67-12-1968 1264-5; cf. page 82.

Stricter Control by UGC: *VC Rep.* 1967-8. G.Marshall to Lasdun on cheap residences: 30-3-

1967. Allowances not announced: *VC Rep* 1967-8. UEA. University Plain Development Plan. Statement by Lasdun 29-7-1966 (Est Lasdun File mid-60s). Marshall, old ways: Comm. Relationship with the Architect 13-11-1968. Money not spent: ibid. 7-10- 1968. Lasdun ... did not make it his job ...: int. Lasdun 1996. 'Lasdun never understood ...': int. J.Macfarlane 1995. 'The breakdown ...': Comm. Relationsh. Architect 7-10-1968. Feilden claim '...wasted £ 500': *Mandate* 13-2-1969. Lasdun quotes / summary of in Comm. Relationsh. Architect 13-11-1968. L.Brett in *AR* 10-1963 263. M.Cassidy, 'Architecture ...': *UQ* vol 18 no 4, 9-1964 362. J. Rykwert, *Zodiac* 18 (1968) 61-3. Birks 74. FT, 'Lasdun and Development Plan', typescript 1996. On university building committees generally: G.C.Moodie & R.Eustace, *Power and Authority in British Universties*, 1974, 107 ff.

LASDUN'S UEA IN THE NATIONAL AND INTERNATIONAL ARCHITECTURAL PRESS: *Architectural Design* 6-1965 288-91; *AJ* 3-3-1965 527-9; *Official Architecture and Planning* 4-1968 513-5; *Arup Journal* 3-1968 36-41; *Concrete Quarterly* 10/12- 1969 18-25; *Architectural Design* 5-1969 245-68; *AR* 4-1970 263-6; F.Hawes, 'UEA Revisit', *Concrete Quarterly Spring* 1990 8-11; S.Upjohn and A.F.Crawshaw, 'Case Study UEA', *AJ* 14-6-1972 1321-38; T.Aldous, 'Adventures in Architecture. The New Universities', *Country Life* 29-1-1976 222-4.

A.H.Th.Vercruysse, 'Plan voor een nieuwe universiteit in Engeland', *Tijdschrift voor architectuur en beeldende kunsten* 10-1965 461-7; *Deutsche Bauzeitung* 1966 470-5; *L'architettura chronache i storia* no.123 1-1966 662-3; *Arkitekten* (Stockholm) 1966 256-60; *Zodiac* 18 (1968) [no page nos]; *Architectural Record* 7-1969 99-110 (see also M.Schmertz, *Campus Planning Design*, New York, 1972); M.Webb, 'Linear Planning in New Universities [Scarborough College, Toronto and UEA], *Country Life Annual* 1969 62-66; C.Dardi, 'Lettura di D.L.', *Lotus* 7 1970 208-235; 'Treppen und Wege der Universitaet von East Anglia', *Werk* 5-1971 300-302; W.Curtis, 'D.Lasdun and his place in the Modern Tradition', *World Architecture* 14 1991 34-53. Cf. R.Banham, *Megastructure*, 1976 119, 131.

**PAGE 64** For the Seven etc. see Birks, S.Muthesius, *The Post-war University. Utopianist*

*Campus and College, 2000.*

**PAGE 70** Cf. R.Banham, *The New Brutalism. Ethic or Aesthetic*, 1966; M.Glendinning & S.Muthesius, *Tower Block*, 1994 Chs. 10, 11, 22, 24. 'Natural concrete...' Lasdun,. Development Plan 1969 33. '80-20 grey ...' Lasdun letter 1997. 'Lasdun: 'will weather ...': *T* 24-3-1975. 'Systems' see *AR* 10-1963 264. D.Osborne, 'University of East Anglia Student Residences,' *Arup Journal* 3-1968 36-41; *Concrete Quarterly* Oct./Dec. 1969 18-25; P.L.Young, 'Pre-cast concrete', *East Anglian Daily Times* 12-11-1968; A.E.J.Morris, *Pre-Cast Concrete in Architecture* 1978 334-6. Generally see: W.Haeberli, *Beton Konstruktion und Form*, Stuttgart 1960; *AJ* 8-8-1962 387-402; P.Marsh, 'When the Going was Good', *Concrete* 10-1972 22-5; K.Bonacker, *Beton. Ein Baustoff wird Schlagwort*, Marburg 1996.

**PAGE 74** 'Encounters...every moment....': *UEA Bulletin* Feb. 1975 12. Lasdun metereology: *Lasdun, Development Plan* 1969 26. Curtis (1994) 95-6. J.M.Richards, *THES* 3-10-1975 6. '25 % of car users...' *Lasdun, Development Plan* 1969 43. Ove Arup & Ptrs., UEA. *Preliminary Report Traffic Problems*, August 1967. Letter from M. Brawne 2000.

**PAGE 76** 'Pirates... ': in letter by P.Smithson to author 2000.

**PAGE 78** R.Dober, *The New Campus in Britain. ...*, New York 1965 9.

**PAGE 80** 'Amenity...' 1964 Library Brief. Lasdun on Computer Centre Extension, remark to authors

**PAGE 82** Letters Univ. to Lasdun 29-6-1967; Lasdun to FT 12-12-1967 (Estates Archives File Lasdun mid 1960s).

**PAGE 84** Smithsons 'could it be...' A.&P.Smithson, *Without Rhetoric*, 1973 34. 'The stepped section ...' AA (1967) 41. E.Cullinan, ment. in *RIBA Journal* 6-1965 273; int. Cullinan 2000. UEA Academic Planning Board Student Residences as a Factor in the Development Plan - Paper II 15th February 1962 filed with Minutes Residences Subcommittee 13-1-1964/21-9-1964. High costs: TES 6-12-1968 1264-5.'Own front door': THES 12-3-1976 6 684. Study Bedrooms: Council Minutes 21-9-1964. Costs: Council Minutes 21-9-1964.

**PAGES 93-101** Cf. P.Greenhalgh (ed.), *Modernism in Design*, 1990; M.Glendinning & S.Muthesius, *Tower Block* 1994, Chs. 1, 15. On 'Welfare State

Architecture': A.Saint, *Towards a Social Architecture. The Role of School Building in post-war England*, 1987, cf. A.Saint, *The Image of the Architect*, 1983. W.Nash, *Rhetoric*, Oxford 1989; A.Kahn (ed.) *Drawing/Building/Text*, Princeton 1991. R.Furnaux-Jordan, 'Denys Lasdun: England': *Canadian Architect* 9-1962 55-64. B.Spence, 'Building a New University', in D.Daiches, *The Idea of a New University. An Experiment at Sussex*, 1964 201-215. Lord James on York: *AJ* 11-3-1964 568; A.Saint, *Social Architecture, op. cit.* 214-22. FT; 'exposition': int. 1966; 'Lasdun good at persuasion' [at the National Theatre]: D.Sudjic, *The Guardian* 6-2-1997. 'Talks with conviction...': *T* 24-3-1975. 'Patrons and committees ...': Helen Smith, 'The Concrete Reality', *Spectator* 14-8-1976 19. Lasdun on clients 1965 RIBA Lecture 'An Architect's Approach to Architecture': *RIBA Journal* 4-1965 185; also in Curtis (1994) 217-19. 'Academic growing points': Birks 74. 'Disciplines...': *Zodiac* 18 (1968) [no p. nos.]. 'Human experience...': D.Lasdun and J.H.V.Davies, 'Thoughts in Progress', *AD* 12-1957 quoted in Curtis (1994). '3 criteria ...': *B* 3-5-1963 876. 'Poetics...': int. Lasdun 1995. A & P. Smithson, *Ordinariness and Light*, 1970; K.Lynch, *The Image of the City*, 1960. 'Landlocked harbour': *Sunday Times* 1-10-1967. 'Urban landscape': *AD* 5-1969 248. 'Map of': quoted in Curtis (1994) 95. 'Walkways...' *Zodiac* 18 (1968) [no p.nos.]. Lasdun: Undercrofts: AA (1967) 41. Lasdun and Models: *AR* 9-1971 148; John R Taylor, *Model Building for Architects and Engineers*, New York 1971; R.Janke, *Architectural Models*, 1978. Einzig hired by Lasdun and Stirling, *Building Design* 22-10-1976. R.Elwall, *Photography takes Command, The Camera and British Architecture 1890-1939* (publ. RIBA 1994).

**PAGES 102-112** Cf.generally: C.J.Crouch, *Student Revolt in Britain*, 1970. 'Dream exposed as sham': *Observer* 19-5-1968; 'beyond redemption': *Colchester Express* 23-5-1974; close Essex: Wivenhoe The Newspaper of the University of Essex 2 16, 17-2-1977, referring to editorial: 'Shut down Essex', *ST* 13-2-1977 16; [Colchester] *Evening Gazette* 7-2-1977. 'Redrawing the map... failed': P.Wilby, 'Interesting experiments but no radical change': *THES* 18-6-1976 6. Norwich weather: Birks 82. 'Idea of a single institution ...': P.Wilby, *THES* 18-6-1976 9. 'Not too litle thought ...': *AJ* 13-12-1972.1349; cf. 'We have tried too hard ...': *EDP* 17-3-1972 (review of Birks). 'Only cemeteries ...': P.Wilby, *THES* 18-6-1976 6. 'Some assume ...': *VC Rep.* 1967-8. Wilby, op. cit. THES 12-3-1976 6-7. 'Lack of fire ...': *Mandate* 11-6-1968. 'We quit': *EEN* 20-5-1968. Interviews 1996, 1997 with students of the late 1960s: Robert Haynes, C.Hewlett; Marcelle Steller-Caudley, Marjorie Allthorp-Guyton and others. Cf. 'Self consious sense...; intellectual gang-bang....': Ruth Feavyour in *Harper's and Queen's* 6-1973 103. 'Hated ...': G. Darley, Visions, Prospects and Compromises', *Higher Education Quarterly* Autumn 1991 362. 'Dinosaur ...': Birks 75; cf. M.Beloff, *The Plateglass Universities*, 1968 110. 'Lasdun's buildings ...'. 'In many important ways ...': Robert Hutchinson & Roger Osborne, 'The Failure of UEA', *Mandate* Jan. 1970. 'The exisiting university structure ...': R. Haynes in *Mandate* Nov. 1969. 'The strange kind of plan ...': int. R.Haynes 1996. Sheila Upjohn and A.F.Crawshaw, 'Case Study: University of East Anglia', *AJ* 14-6-1972 1321-1338; 'bad campus plan ...': *Guardian* 31-5-1971. Parking: idea to pay ....*VC Rep.* for 1968-9.

Looking for new planner: Comm. Relat. Arch. 29-10-1968. On Feilden: S.Marks (ed.), *Concerning Buildings. Studies in Honour of Sir Bernard Feilden*, 1996, it does not mention UEA. Feilden, FT, Lasdun: Memo FT 25-11-1968, int. FT 1996. 'I admire Lasdun ...': int. Feilden 1995. New cost limits ...: Comm. Relation with the Architect. 25-10-1968. Broad: *VC Rep.* 1971-2, *EDP* 22-5-1979, *VC Rep.* 1978-9. Conservation, Park, Prospect, Artificial Mount: *EDP* 31-12-1974; *EEN* 8-9-1978. Geometrical Bridge given by and built by Atlas Agregates. R.Reich (Consultant Landscape Architect to Feilden & Mawson), 'The Broad...', *Landscape Design* 1980 14-18. 1968 appointment Brenda Colvin landscape architect.

'I take account of contexts ...': int. Feilden 1995. 'University has been without a heart': *VC Rep.* 1971-2. 'Walking briskly': *AJ* 14-6-1972 1330, 1335. Feilden Report A 'Inflation in the Building Industry'; Report B 'The Use of Blockwork' (UEA Estates Archives), 1974. 'Energy crisis... cuts ...':'... strikes, chaos: *VC Rep.* 1973-4. 'All buildings finished ...': *EDP* 2-10-1975. 'University has come of age ...':*VC Rep.* 1972-3. 'Main attraction ...': *EEN* 9-5-1975.

**PAGES 113-125** 'The town square of our community': *VC Rep.* 1972-3; *AJ* 13-12-1972 1349. Mackintosh Hall project: *VC Rep.* 1968-9; *Mandate* 13-2-1969; P.W.Penn, 'A New University Plan', *Mandate* [n.d.] c. May 1970]; Development Plan II April 1970. Restaurant and Café: *AJ* 14-6-1972 1336. Chaplaincy: *EDP* 20-1-1970, *EDP* 21-1-1972; B.J.Banyard [Interior Designer with F& M], 'Interior Design at the UEA', *Interior Design* 11-1972 772. Shops not allowed on fringes: *T* 19-6-1963; *EDP* 15-6-1963.

Sports Hall: *VC Rep.* 1970-1, 1971-2; *Consulting Engineer* 8-1971.

The Registry and Council House ('Senate'): *VC Rep.* 1971-2, 1973-4; *EDP* 2-10-1975; *AJ* 8-10-1975 721; *AJ* 10-10-1975. UEA/F&M *Design Report Senate House* [n.d., c. 1972]; UEA/F&M *Design Report Council House* (1972); *Building* 3-10-75; *Precast Concrete* 2-1976; *Building Design* 13-2-1976. On Benney see T.Harrod, *The Crafts in Britain in the 20th century,* 1998, Chapter 10. Sports Centre 'splendid place ...': *VC Rep.* 1971-2. 'Theatricality ...': int. FT 1996. Carter against pomp: *Listener* 5-5-1966. 'High culture and haute ...': M. Beloff, *The Plateglass Universities*, 1968 186. 'There is no student objection ...': Birks, p.32. Horsham Z Block: *AR* 4-1970 290. Wolfson/Orwell 'Site A Plans', 3-1973, 11-1973.

Music Centre: Scheme Design Report Nov. 1971; Arup appointed 1970; £80 000 Nuffield Grant building and equipment, UGC £38.000; *VC Rep.* 1971-2; delayed to May/Oct.1973, openend *AR* 3-1975 131-139; *Baumeister* 9-1975 784-6. Dowson Gold Medal; *EDP* 15-10-1981. Research Park: Brawne *AR* 4-1970 308. IFR *AJ* 11-2-1970 349-362. I owe thanks to: E.Stratton, R.Gill, G.Aldous, J.Richardson, C.Reynolds, G.Jones, D.Sang.

**IV PAGES 126-137 BEGINNINGS**
See generally: S.Muthesius, *The Post-War University. Utopianist Campus and College*, 2000; M.Beloff, *The Plateglass Universities*, 1968; H.Perkin, *New Universities in the United Kingdom (Studies on Innovation in Higher Education)* OECD Paris 1969. 'Paper 48/60: 'New University Institutions' PRO UGC 2 60. 'Dinsaur': Birks 75. 'Citadel': S.Lyall, '.... Essex', *New Society* 16-9-1982 467. 'Robbins Report': Committee on Higher Education, *Higher Education* (under chairmanship of Lord Robbins, *Parliamentary*

*Papers*, Cmnd 2154), 1964.

'1/3 numbers, 2/3 ideas': P.Wilby, 'Interesting Experiments but no radical change', *THES* 18-6-1976 6; 'experiments': see M.Beloff, *The Plateglass Universities*, 1968. State proportion: A.H.Halsey, 'The Universities and the State', *UQ* vol. 23 no. 2 Spring 1969 128-48 (138). 'Good' academic staff: 'Sites chosen to attract dons?', *Observer* 21-5-1961. 'Hands on ...': M.Shattock, *The UGC and the Management of British Universities*, Buckingham 1994. 'De facto control ...'. 'The alliance ...': A.H.Halsey, 'The Universties and the State', UQ vol. 23 no. 2 Spring 1969 (143). 'Born Free': quoted in: M.Beloff, *The Plateglass Universities*, 1968 26.

University graduates ...': K.Amis, 'Lone voices....', *Encounter* 15-7-1960 6-11. 'Redrawing the map ...': A.Briggs, 'Universities for Tomorrow. Maps of Learning', *New Statesman* 3-3-1961 338-340. "New" *Listener* 11-11 1965 747. 'What is the Modern equivalent ...': 'The Design of New Universities', *RIBA Journal* 7-1964 301-9 (308). 'New University Movement... cathedrals ...': *AA* (1967) 7. L.Brett, 'Universities Today', *AR* 10-1957 225, 240-251. William Stone Building for Peterhouse, by L Martin and C.St.J.Wilson: P.Booth & N.Taylor, *Cambridge New Architecture*, 1970 39-41.

NORWICH Kate Wharton (in 'Family Forum' on Norwich and York) *Daily Telegraph* 29-11-1963. 'We are a truly regional university': *VC Rep.*1964-5; cf. VC in *EDP* 10-5-1967. Cf. W.G.V.Balchin, 'University Expansion in GB', *New Scientist* 12-3-1959 582-5; FT, The Founding of UEA, *A Reminiscent Chronicle*, November 1963 (typescript). Harold Vincent Viscount Mackintosh, Obituary *T* 29-12-1964. On some important local names: *Mandate* 1970 [n.d., c. May]. 'Mackintosh... warm ...': Int.Colman 1996. Appeal figures and bet: *EEN* 11-12-1962 etc. 'College': G Tilsley, *A Personal Reminiscences* 1988 68 (Library Archive); Report Promotion Committee 1960-2, 8-1960; PRO UGC 7 212 Letter Wilson 18-5-1960, 27-5-1960.

Norfolk Academics: Letter Ron. S.Edwards to Sir K Murray 10-2-1960: PRO UGC 7 174. On FT: *T* 26-8-1961. '100 barnstorming speeches...': int. FT 1996. 'Against the advice ...': int FT 1996. 'Foster academic community ...': *EDP* 28-3-1963; *EEN* 28-3-1963.

**PAGES 138-142** Village: Site given by the Gurneys. *ABN* 27-11-1963 877-80; *Surveyor* 2-11-1963 1361-64; *Building Industry News* 4-4-1963; *DailyTelegraph* 29-11-1963; *TES* 21-2-1964 437; *B* 28-10-1963; *Interbuild* 10-1963; *Construction and Labour News* 30-10-1963; *Illustrated London News* 23-7-1966 15; *Medway*. Issued by Medway Buidling Supplies Ltd. Rochester Kent No. 3 Autumn 1963. *VC Rep.* 1962-3 etc.; Birks 75-6. For Norwich Council Housing and the issue of prefabrication see M.Horsey and S.Muthesius, *Provincial Mixed Development*, Norwich 1986

University Buildings Comm. Minutes 5-12-1962, 19-3-1963, 10-1-1963 (Estates Archive). 'Mawson easy ....': int. Rowan Hare 1997.

P. Lubbock, Earlham, 1922; *VC Rep* 1961-2 7; PRO UGC 7 440 Paper 143/63 17-10-1963; Council Minutes 7-12-1964. Tilsley letter from America: int. Tilsley 1996. 'It seemed desirable ...': PRO UGC 7 440 memo 17-7-1963. Wood Hall: A. Longcroft, *Wood Hall Hethersett, Historical Survey*, Norwich 1995; cf. O Chadwick, *Victorian Miniature. The Lives of William Wayte Andrew and Sir John Boileau at Ketteringham Norfolk*, 1960.

Site: PRO UGC 7 212; Tilsley, Personal Reminiscences (typescript) 1988 76ff. (83). Submission of Executive Comm. 10-11-1959; R.G.Jobling, 'The location and siting of a new university', *UQ* Spring 1970 123-136. 'A university from the grain ...': *TES* 6-2-1959 218. 'Greater social ...': *AJ* 19-5-1960 744-5. 'Dreaming spires ...': int. Colman 1996. 'Dismal and unattractive ...': G.Tilsley, *A Personal Reminiscence*, 1988 83 (Library Archive).

**V PAGES 143-156 PATRONAGE**
Quoted from Virginia Woolf's Journals (*A Passionate Apprentice: The Early Journals*, 1990) in P.Tolhurst, *East Anglia, A Literary Pigrimage*, Bungay 1996 120. I.Nairn, 'Britain's Changing Cities'. Norwich: Regional capital', *Listener* 13-8-1964 226-7, 310; cf. I.Nairn *Britain's Changing Towns*, 1967 162-9. 'Lodging Gaps ....': *T* 4-8-1963 10. Cf. Eastern Daily Press (publ. by), *A Norfolk Century*, Norwich 1999. 'Dominant factor ...'; 'the state effectively ...': I.Cullen & S.Major, 'Uniting Town and Gown', *THES* 8-2-1974 13; cf. their book The University in an Urban Environment, 1974. 'Tweedy provincialism ...': *AR* 12-1978 355-

6. Cf. M.Yorke, *The Spirit of the Place. Nine Neo-Romantic Artists and their Times*, 1988. N.Pevsner, *The Englishness of English Art*, 1956 172 ff.. S.Hardingham, *England. A Guide to recent Architecture*, 1995 182. G.Nobbs, *Norwich City Hall*, Norwich 1988. W.Harrod (&S.Linnell), *Norfolk*,1957. Lasdun 'magnificent site...' Letter 4-1-1962 (Est F/N 213). 'Studied site for a year ...': *EDP* 2-12-1968. 'Careful surveys...calibrated...' int. Lasdun. 'Harbour ...': *ABN* 1-5-1965 647; *AA* (1967) 40. 'West Norwich indebted...': *VC Rep.* 1968/9. Eventual suburban development: M Brawne in *AR* 4-1970 308; *OAP* 4- 1968 513. Open to public, 'cordon sanitaire ...': Lasdun lecture *RIBA Journal* 4-1965; *Lasdun Development Plan* 1969 54, 116-7. See C. Gibson *A Natural History of UEA*, Norwich (UEA Biology School 1987). 'Norwich got what it wanted': *AJ* 14-6-1972 1321. On Local Government... , *Town and Country Planning* 6-1968. W.Harrod, *op. cit.* 41. CF. Pevsner's *Buildings of England, Norfolk I*, new ed. by Bill Wilson (1997) opts for the vernacular in Norfolk (170).

**ON UEA's HISTORY GENERALLY:**

M.Sanderson, *A History of the University of East Anglia 1918-2000*, forthcoming. FT, 'UEA', in M.G.Ross (ed.), *New Universities in the modern World*, 1966 53-68; *AA* (1967) 36-43. FT, *Doing Different in a Cold Climate. The St. John's College Lecture* 25-10-1988 (publ. Cambridge 1988).

**ILLUSTRATION SOURCES**

(No sources given: author; MBJ: Michael Brandon Jones; WAM: School of World Art Studies UEA). Sources have been tracked down to the best of our knowledge. If anything has been overlooked please get in touch with the author at UEA, Sainsbury Centre. General: all plans by the Lasdun firm are their copyright and are reproduced with permission. AD: John Wiley & Sons Limited. Reproduced with permission.
*8* MBJ. *10* B 3-5-1963 875; The Photographic Co. Norwich. *13* UEA. *15* MBJ. *16* The architects/UEA. *17* UEA. *18* AJ 15-6-1995 *33*; *Casabella* 6-1995 *59* (right). *19* MBJ (interior). *20* UEA/Mather, *Design Reports* 1991, Mather Drawing: R.Mather. *22* AJ 5-3-1986 *34*. *24* UEA. *25* AJ 5-3-1986 *33*. *26* AR 11-1985 *103*. *29* UEA. *31* UEA. *32 33* WAM. *37* UEA. *38* Catalogue of Sainsbury Collection, Exhibtion... April 1978 (publ. by UEA / A.Zwemmer Ltd.). *39* UEA. *40* AD 2-1979. *43 44 45* WAM. *46* N.Foster. John Kingsley. *47* N.Foster (Photo Richard Davies). *51 EEN* 25-4-1963. *59* UEA. *63 New Society* 16-5-1963 8. *64 65 AR* 4-1970. *66* Curtis (1994). *67* B 3-5-1963 875. *68 69* D.Lasdun & Ptrs.; UEA. *71* UEA *Lasdun Development Plan* 1969. *72* UEA *Lasdun Development Plan* 1969; Eastern Counties Newspapers (Charles Nicholson). *73* UEA. *74* UEA Estates Archive. *75* UEA; *TES* 6-12-1968. *76* illustr. in var. public. by the Smithsons, Copyright Peter Smithson. *77* J.Prest, The Illustrated History of Oxford, Oxford 1993. *78 Lasdun Development Plan* 1969. *79* UEA. *80* MBJ; Lasdun Development Plan 1969. *82 83* UEA Estates Archive. *85* Martin: *AD* 9-1965 433; CPB: *AR* 1-1961 *11*; Lasdun Cambridge: *Zodiac 18* (1968); Lasdun St. John's: *Canadian Architect* 9-1962 *69*. *86* UEA. *87* Bedroom, Sunroof: Curtis (1994); Kitchen: UEA. *89* UEA. *90 91* Birks; Curtis (1994); A.Saint, *Change of Heart ...*, Crown Copyright NMR 1992; BBC; *Sunday Times* 15-1-1978 (Magazine); UEA. *95 Building* 4-3-1977 *51*. *99* AR 4-1970 264/*Building Design* 22-10-1976. Curtis (1994). *100 101* UEA. *106* (top) Eastern Counties Newspapers Norwich; Mandate [UEA] c. late 1969. *107* UEA/Lasdun (also in EDP 5-10-1966); *T* 29-4-1971; UEA. *109 EDP* 17-1-1969. *111* AJ 20-11-1974 1197. *113 114 115* UEA. *116 EDP* 3-7-1973. *117* Feilden & Mawson *Reports Senate House, Council House* 1973; UEA; MBJ. *118* Queen: *EDP* 25-5-1968; Dress: *EDP* 22-4-1966. *119* UEA. *120* Z plan: *AR* 4-1970 290; *121* Horsham: UEA; Waveney *EEN* 7-4-1972; Orwell: Plans... 1973.*122 123* UEA; *Music Centre Scheme Design Report*, 11-1971. *124* The Photographic Co. Norwich. *125* (IFR) UEA. *133 EDP* 17-5-1962. *137* UEA. *138 Daily Telegraph* 29-11-63. *139* UEA. *140* Aylsham: MBJ. *141* UEA. *142 Ordnance Survey* Map 1960s; PRO UGC 7 212. *144* Castle Museum Norwich. Norfolk Museum Services. *147* I.Nairn, *Britain's Changing Towns*, 1967. *150* City of Norwich / Sarah Cocke. *151* Norwich City Hall. Map: UEA / SM.

**ARCHITECTURAL AND BUILDING AWARDS**

| | |
|---|---|
| Denys Lasdun | 1969 |
| Civic Trust - UEA Stage 1 | |
| | |
| Feilden & Mawson | 1972 |
| Civic Trust - The Square | |
| | |
| Arup Associates | 1973 |
| Norfolk Association of Architects Craftsmanship Award - Music Centre Blockwork | |
| | |
| Arup Associates | 1974 |
| RIBA Eastern Region - Music Centre | |
| | |
| Foster Associates | 1978 |
| RIBA Eastern Region - Sainsbury Centre | |
| | |
| Foster Associates | 1978 |
| Finniston Award - Sainsbury Centre structural steelwork | |
| | |
| Foster Associates | 1979 |
| RS Reynolds (AIA) - Sainsbury Centre | |
| | |
| Foster Associates | 1979 |
| British Tourist Board Special Award - Sainsbury Centre, for private enterprise | |
| | |
| UEA Estates Office | 1979 |
| RICS Conservation - The Broad | |
| | |
| Foster Associates | 1980 |
| Ambrose Congreave - Sainsbury Centre | |
| | |
| Foster Associates | 1980 |
| British Tourist Board Museum of the Year - Sainsbury Centre | |
| | |
| Foster Associates | 1980 |
| 6th International prize Brussels - Sainsbury Centre | |
| | |
| UEA Estates Office | 1980 |
| Civic Trust - The Broad | |

| | |
|---|---|
| Rick Mather | 1985 |
| Architectural Design - Climatic Research Unit | |
| | |
| Rick Mather | 1988 |
| RIBA Eastern Region - Education, Computing Science and Climatic Research Unit | |
| | |
| Foster Associates | 1991 |
| British Construction Industry Award (runner up) - SCVA Crescent Wing | |
| | |
| Sir Norman Foster and Partners | 1992 |
| Design Review Minerva Award (shortlist) - SCVA Crescent Wing | |
| | |
| Sir Norman Foster and Partners | 1992 |
| RIBA Eastern Region - SCVA Crescent Wing | |
| | |
| Sir Norman Foster and Partners | 1992 |
| Civic Trust - SCVA Crescent Wing | |
| | |
| Rick Mather | 1994 |
| RIBA Eastern Region - Constable Terrace | |
| | |
| John Miller and Partners | 1994 |
| RIBA Eastern Region - Queens Building | |
| | |
| John Miller and Partners | 1994 |
| RIBA National Award for 1994 - Queens Building | |
| | |
| Rick Mather | 1995 |
| Civic Trust - Constable Terrace | |
| | |
| John Miller and Partners | 1995 |
| RIBA Eastern Region - Elizabeth Fry Building | |
| | |
| John Miller and Partners | 1997 |
| Civic Trust - Queens / Elizabeth Fry | |
| | |
| John Miller and Partners | 1999 |
| Building Services Journal Probe Award - Elizabeth Fry Building | |

# Index

# ARCHITECTS AT THE UNIVERSITY OF EAST ANGLIA TO 1995

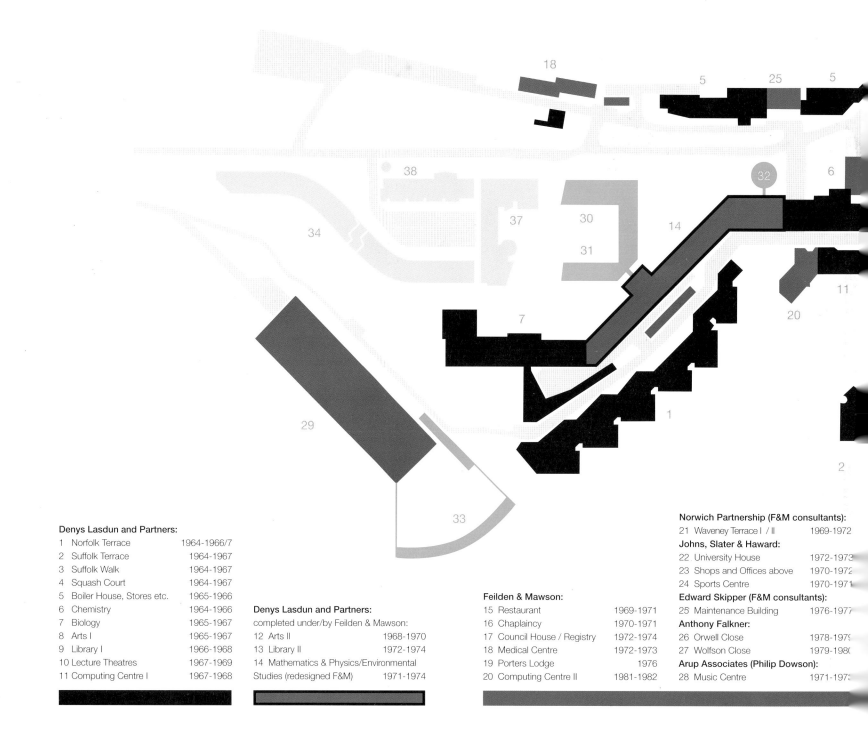

**Denys Lasdun and Partners:**

| 1 | Norfolk Terrace | 1964-1966/7 |
|---|---|---|
| 2 | Suffolk Terrace | 1964-1967 |
| 3 | Suffolk Walk | 1964-1967 |
| 4 | Squash Court | 1964-1967 |
| 5 | Boiler House, Stores etc. | 1965-1966 |
| 6 | Chemistry | 1964-1966 |
| 7 | Biology | 1965-1967 |
| 8 | Arts I | 1965-1967 |
| 9 | Library I | 1966-1968 |
| 10 | Lecture Theatres | 1967-1969 |
| 11 | Computing Centre I | 1967-1968 |

**Denys Lasdun and Partners:**
completed under/by Feilden & Mawson:

| 12 | Arts II | 1968-1970 |
|---|---|---|
| 13 | Library II | 1972-1974 |
| 14 | Mathematics & Physics/Environmental Studies (redesigned F&M) | 1971-1974 |

**Feilden & Mawson:**

| 15 | Restaurant | 1969-1971 |
|---|---|---|
| 16 | Chaplaincy | 1970-1971 |
| 17 | Council House / Registry | 1972-1974 |
| 18 | Medical Centre | 1972-1973 |
| 19 | Porters Lodge | 1976 |
| 20 | Computing Centre II | 1981-1982 |

**Norwich Partnership (F&M consultants):**

| 21 | Waveney Terrace I / II | 1969-1972 |
|---|---|---|

**Johns, Slater & Haward:**

| 22 | University House | 1972-1973 |
|---|---|---|
| 23 | Shops and Offices above | 1970-1972 |
| 24 | Sports Centre | 1970-1971 |

**Edward Skipper (F&M consultants):**

| 25 | Maintenance Building | 1976-1977 |
|---|---|---|

**Anthony Falkner:**

| 26 | Orwell Close | 1978-1979 |
|---|---|---|
| 27 | Wolfson Close | 1979-1980 |

**Arup Associates (Philip Dowson):**

| 28 | Music Centre | 1971-1973 |
|---|---|---|